Great Cycle Routes
The North and South Downs

Jeremy Evans

Great Cycle Routes
The North and South Downs

Jeremy Evans

The Crowood Press

First published in 1995 by
The Crowood Press Ltd
Ramsbury, Marlborough
Wiltshire SN8 2HR

www.crowood.com

This impression 2008

British Library Cataloguing-in-Publication Data
A catalogue record for this book is available from the British Library.

ISBN 978 1 85223 850 6

Photographs by Jeremy Evans
Map-drawings by Dave Ayres

Reproduced from Ordnance Survey mapping
on behalf of Her Majesty's Stationery Office,
© Crown Copyright 10038003 2005.

Printed and bound in Spain by GraphyCems

Contents

Introduction..7

The South Downs 19

Ride 1: Chichester to Petworth 20
Ride 2: Stoughton and Harting Downs...................25
Ride 3: From Petworth to Bramber 28
Ride 4: Around Haywards Heath 32
Ride 5: The South Downs Way..................................36
Ride 6: From Queen Elizabeth Country Park..........44
Ride 7: Kingley Vale and Stansted...........................48
Ride 8: Goodwood and the Downs............................52
Ride 9: Selhurst Park and the Downs 55
Ride 10: Bignor Hill and the Downs.........................58
Ride 11: River Arun Ride...62
Ride 12: Chanctonbury and Cissbury Rings 66
Ride 13: Bramber Castle and the Downs 70
Ride 14: Bramber Castle and the Downs Link 74
Ride 15: Bramber Castle to Wolstonbury Hill.........78
Ride 16: Ditchling Beacon and the Downs 82
Ride 17: Firle Beacon and the Downs 86
Ride 18: Alfriston and the Downs 90

The North Downs 95

Ride 19: The Downs Link 96
Ride 20: The Devil's Punchbowl..............................100
Ride 21: Guildford and the Downs Westward.........104
Ride 22: Guildford to Leith Hill..............................107
Ride 23: Hatchlands and the Downs 112
Ride 24: Polesden Lacey and the Downs 116
Ride 25: Box Hill and the Downs.............................120

Introduction

RIDE INFORMATION

Area: Where the ride is located.

OS Map: The relevant OS Landranger 1:50 000 map for the route.

Route: Waymarks from start to finish, with OS grid reference numbers. All of the rides in this book bar the South Downs Way are circular, making it possible to start at a number of locations.

Nearest BR Stations: Most of the routes are accessible from a railway station. Owing to the market-led policies of British Rail which have become extremely bike-unfriendly, it is necessary to check restrictions and costs before you start and board a train.

Approx Length: In miles and kilometres. There should always be some allowance for getting lost or altering the route.

Time: This is very difficult to assess, and will depend on factors such as whether the tracks are dry, how many hills have to be climbed, how fast you ride, and how many pubs and places of interest there are en route.

Rating: An 'Easy' ride should be accessible for riders of all abilities, excluding sub-teenage children; a 'Moderate' ride may prove harder in terms of terrain, length, hills, churning those pedals, and possibly navigation; a 'Hard' ride is best suited to experienced offroad riders with a high level of commitment. However these ratings can be changed by the weather – for instance an 'Easy' ride in very dry weather may become a 'Hard' ride when the tracks are churned to mud.

Places to Visit / Top Pubs: Virtually all of these rides feature a number of possible pub stops. I have also indicated cafes and other facilities to enjoy along the route.

Stick to the rules, and you won't get into trouble!

COMMON SENSE OFFROAD

The tracks and trails used for offroad cycling must be shared. The basic problem for mountain bikers is that bikes are generally so much faster than walkers and horse-riders. That is the principal factor which causes antagonism, but why hurry? Why not take it easy and enjoy the ride? Stick to the following common sense rules, and everyone should be happy.

DANGER
DO NOT LEAVE THIS ROAD
DO NOT TOUCH ANYTHING
IT MAY EXPLODE AND KILL YOU

Be safe! Don't ride into danger.

1. Stay on public bridleways, byways or roads. Never ride on footpaths. Cycling on private tracks or open ground is not usually allowed without permission from the land owner. Always moderate your speed.

2. When you ride offroad, the bridleways and byways are classified as 'Highways'. This means the Highway Code applies, and you can be prosecuted for riding dangerously, especially if you are involved in an accident. Any form of racing is illegal on a public highway, unless it is a specially organized event and permission has been obtained. Byways may also be shared with motorized vehicles. They should give way to cyclists, but as when meeting any vehicle, it is necessary to play safe.

3. Learn how to prevent skids and ride with control to help prevent erosion, especially in the wet. If it is very wet, it is much better to push or carry your bike. Going off the official tracks and trails can cause unnecessary erosion, as well as damaging plant and animal environments.

4. When you meet other people offroad and in the countryside, be courteous and considerate. Always slow right down and give way to both walkers and horse-riders, even if it means dismounting and lifting your bike out of the way. Bikes are almost silent, so give warning of your approach in as polite a manner as possible. The British Horse Society would like you to 'Hail a Horse'; we think the very best policy is to come to a complete halt until the animals have passed you by. If you are riding in a group, all go to one side of the track. Take particular care when you ride past children – you may not worry them, but you may terrorize/infuriate their parents.

5. Make sure your bike is safe to ride, and won't let you down in the middle of nowhere on a fast downhill – learn basic maintenance and take essential spares. In the interests of safety take drink and food, and wear suitable clothing for the weather conditions and length of ride. It is wise to wear a helmet, putting a layer of polystyrene between your cranium and any hard object in the unlikely event of a bad fall particularly on-road.

6. To avoid getting lost, it is always wise to carry a compass and relevant map such as the OS 1:50, 000 Landranger series. You should know where you are, and have the ability to re-plan the route and cut the ride short.

7. Follow the Country Code. Leave nothing behind – no litter, no orange peel, the minimum of noise, no bad memories for yourself or for others, and if possible not even a sign of your wheeltracks. Always shut gates behind you (unless they should obviously be left open). Don't blast through fields of cows or sheep – neither they nor the farmer will like it. If you ride with a dog for a companion, be sure to keep it under control.

Ride together, but give way to walkers.

USE THAT MAP!

Unless the route is very easy or you know it well, you should never ride without a map, never ride without a compass. Once you get the hang of it, using them is easy and will ensure you know where you're heading.

A map is a diagram which shows the features of an area of land such as mountains, hills, woods, rivers, railways, roads, tracks, towns and buildings. All these and many other features are shown by special signs that map readers can understand. There is always a table on the map which explains the signs. On a 1:50, 000 map (OS Landranger) 1cm on the map equals 50,000cm on the ground; this equals 2cm for every kilometre, or 1 1/4 in per mile.

THE GRID SYSTEM: Maps are covered by a grid of numbered horizontal and vertical grid lines. The grid is used to find an exact place on a map. To find a grid reference position you read the first three numbers off the vertical grid line which is called the Eastings line. You then read the next three numbers off the horizontal Northings grid line. Where they meet is where you want to be.

CONTOURS: Contours are lines on a map which join areas that are the same height above sea level (in metres). The difference in height between the contour lines is called the vertical height. The closer the lines are the steeper the hill will be. Contour lines are spaced at 10m intervals on 1:50, 000 Landranger maps, and at 5m intervals on 1:25, 000 Outdoor Leisure maps.

It is generally best to arrange your ride so the climbs are short and steep and the descents are long and fast; it is also best to get major climbs out of the way early on the ride. Sometimes it is quite difficult to know if you will be going up or down; a river or stream on the map is a sure sign of dropping down to a valley, but you can also work it out by looking at the contour line height numbers, as the top of the number is always uphill.

Do you know where you're going.

USING A COMPASS: A compass is a valuable aid to finding your way. The most popular style is the Swedish-made Silva on which most modern hiking (equally suitable for biking) compasses are based. It is low in price, light, very tough, and easy to use.

The compass should be carried on a lanyard at all times; in bad visibility it may be the only means you have of finding the way. The compass needle always points to Magnetic North, but keep it away from close contact with any metallic object to which it might be sensitive. Knowing that the needle points North, you can always follow a course in the direction you wish to go. The vertical grid lines on a map point to Grid North; this may be a few degrees different from Magnetic North, but the difference is very small.

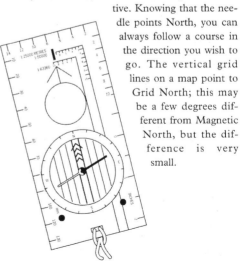

OFFROAD WITH KIDS

Why not take the kids with you? With a little care the whole family can have a great day out, and when the kids are too big for a child seat you can put them in the saddle and still stay in control.

There's no point in taking children cycling on-road or offroad if they don't enjoy it, because then you won't enjoy it. Always follow the three golden rules:

1. Make sure they're comfortable.

2. Keep them amused.

3. Don't bite off more than you can chew.

COMFORT: For a child up to around four years of age, go for the best rear-mounted child seat you can find. It must obviously be secure on the bike, with a high back and sides to help protect its occupant if you should fall, deep footwells to protect the feet, and a full harness to hold the child firmly in; a safety bar for the child to grip on to is also a worthwhile extra. Ideally, the seat should also be quick and easy to put on and take off your bike, so when you ride alone the seat doesn't have to go with you.

It's a good idea to get children used to wearing helmets as early as possible, but with very young children (under one year old) there is a often a problem making the helmet stay on. This results in a miserable baby with a helmet tipped down over its eyes; best then to do without the helmet and be extra careful, until you can be sure it will sit comfortably in position.

Make sure the straps of a helmet are sufficiently tight. Children won't like you fiddling under their chins, and your best policy is to train them to put on and take off the helmet themselves as young as possible, ensuring the straps are adjusted to the right length. Shop around for a child helmet and do ask to try it on. As with most adult helmets, removable rubber pads are used to alter the internal diameter, but the most important consideration is that the design of the helmet and its straps hold it firmly on the head. Some helmets seem to want to slide forward on impact, which is useless.

The child is protected from the headwind by your body, but can still get pretty cold sitting there doing nothing; in winter, an all-in-one waterproof/windproof coverall suit does the job really well. Remember that young children require all sorts of extras – extra clothes, nappies, drink, apples, and so on. Try to keep their requirements down to an acceptable minimum; a neat solution is to carry extras in a small backpack that mounts behind the child seat itself.

A child seat can be a lot of fun.

KEEP THEM HAPPY: Young children generally love riding on the back of bikes, and want to tell you all about what's going on. It can be bad enough understanding them at the best of times, but in this situation it becomes ridiculous and your replies degenerate to a meaningless 'Yes' or 'No'.

With that level of conversation a child will only sit happily in its seat for so long; the duration will obviously be affected by the weather, especially if it's freezing and foul. Children like regular stops if they're to stay happy, so take a stash of little treats – apples, nuts and raisins, and so on – and ensure that you get to the picnic or pub (make sure they allow children) on time with the shortest part of the ride left for the end of the day.

Routes should be chosen with care and an eye on safety. A rock-strewn 'downhill extreme', which is just waiting to throw you over the handlebars, should obviously be avoided. To start with, keep to mellow and easy offroad routes such as those found in the New Forest or an old railway line such as the Downs Link in Sussex. Moderate uphills are all right when the weight of the child helps back wheel traction; immod-

erate uphills are plain stupid, as you wheeze and groan pushing both bike and child together.

What about downhills? As long as you're in control there's no danger in going fast on a smooth track or road. Rather than hitting the brakes, it's better to treat it as a laugh and teach the child to get used to the thrill of safe speed.

There comes a time when children grow too big and bored for a conventional rear-mounted seat, but too young to ride their own bike and keep pace (and keep safe) with adults. One answer is the Trailerbike, a remarkable hybrid, which claims it will take children from four to ten years old with a maximum weight of 42kg (6.5 stone). It allows you to ride with your child; they get all the fun of riding their own bike, but you have total control over their speed, where they go, and ultimately their safety. They can also pedal as much or as little as they like. If they have the muscle and aptitude, they'll help push you uphill as well as down.

The Trailerbike is a hybrid which is excellent as children get older.

Abide by the rules – never ride on footpaths.

OFFROAD RIGHTS OF WAY IN ENGLAND & WALES

PUBLIC BRIDLEWAYS: Open to walkers and horse-riders, and also to cyclists since 1968. This right is not sacrosanct; bike bans are possible if riders are considered to have become too much of a nuisance.

PUBLIC BYWAYS: Usually unsurfaced tracks open to cyclists, walkers, horse-riders and vehicles which have right of access to houses.

PUBLIC FOOTPATHS: No rights to cycle. You probably have the right to push a bike, but the temptation to ride is high and it is best to avoid footpaths whenever possible.

FORESTRY COMMISSION: Access on designated cycle paths, or by permission from the local Forest Manager. At present there is a general presumption in favour of bikes using Forestry land gratis; this may change.

DESIGNATED CYCLE PATHS: Specially built cycle tracks for urban areas; or using Forestry Commission land or railway lines.

PAVEMENTS: Cycling is illegal on pavements. However it is frequently much safer and more pleasant than cycling on the road, and with the proviso that you take great care to avoid pedestrians (who are seldom seen on out-of-town pavements), using pavements can be perfectly reasonable.

WHAT IF BRIDLEWAYS AND BYWAYS ARE BLOCKED?

Cyclists are used to being on the defensive on Britain's roads; offroad they should stand up for their rights. The relevant landowner and local authority have the responsibility to maintain bridleways and byways and ensure they are passable with gates that work. It is illegal for a landowner to block a right of way, close or divert it (only the local authority or central government can do this), or put up a misleading notice to deter you from using it.

It is also illegal to plough up or disturb the surface of a right of way unless it is a footpath or bridleway running across a field. In that case the farmer must make good the surface within twenty-four hours or two weeks if it is the first disturbance for a particular crop. A bridleway so restored must have a minimum width of two metres, and its line must be clearly apparent on the ground. A farmer also has a duty to prevent any crops other than grass making a right of way difficult to follow. A bridleway across crops should have a two metre clear width; a field edge bridleway should have a clear width of three metres.

If you run into difficulty on any of the above, you can file a complaint with the Footpaths Officer at the local council, giving full details of the offence and a precise map reference of where it occurred.

Some bridleways are more difficult to follow than others!

OFFROAD CARE AND REPAIR

Have you decided on your route, got the right OS map, and your compass? Have you got all the right clothes – ready for rain, wind or sun – plus food and sufficient drink if it's going to be hot? That just leaves your bike, so don't risk getting let down by a breakdown.

Always prepare your bike carefully.

BRAKE CHECK: The most important part of your bike – if the brakes fail, you could be dead. Check the blocks for wear, turn them or change them as necessary. Lubricate the cables, check they won't slip, and if there is any sign of fraying, change them. Lube the brake pivots – if the spring return on the brakes isn't working well, they will need to be stripped down and cleaned.

WHEELS: Check your tyres for general wear and side-wall damage; look for thorns. If a wheel is out of line or dented, it needs to be adjusted with a spoke key; also check for loose spokes. Always carry a pump and a puncture repair kit.

CHAIN CARE: Give your chain a regular lube – there are all sorts of fancy spray lubes around, some of which cost a lot of money; however, although the more universal sorts are cheap and reliable, they do attract the dirt. If your chain and cogs are manky, clean them with a rag soaked in spray lubricant or a special 'chain bath'; adjust stiff links with a chain breaker, which is a useful tool to carry.

MOVING PARTS: Clean and lube the derailleur jockey wheels and gear cogs. Lube the freewheel with the bike on its side. Clean and lube the chainwheel gear mechanism. Lube and check the cables for both sets of gears. Lube the bottom bracket – the most basic method is to pour heavy oil down the top tube. Lube the pedals by taking off the end caps. Check that both the cranks and headset are tight. Check that the derailleur lines up properly.

Other things that may go wrong include breaking the chain or having a cable slip, though if you take care of your bike these occurrences are very rare. Just in case, however, it is wise to carry a chainlink extractor, which rejoins a broken chain, 4/5/6mm Allen keys, a small adjustable spanner, and a screwdriver with both a flat head and a Phillips head. The neat solution is a 'multi-tool' which includes all these items in one package.

PUNCTURE REPAIR

The most common offroad repair is a puncture and the most common cause is the hawthorn. To cope with this you need a pump, tyre levers and a puncture repair kit; you may also like to carry a spare tube. Always go for a full-size pump with the correct valve fitting; the pump should fit inside the frame, ideally on the down tube. A double-action pump puts in the air fastest.

Two tyre levers are sufficient, either in plastic or metal, whilst a spare tube saves the hassle of finding the leak and doing a patch offroad – unless you puncture twice.

1. Stop as soon as you feel a tyre go soggy: riding on a flat tyre is asking for trouble. Find a suitable place to do the repair – well away from any cars – and turn the bike upside-down. Take care you know where you put things down: it is too easy to lose that little black screw cap that covers the valve.

2. Undo the brake cable near the brake block, flip off the quick release lever at the hub, and remove the wheel. This is more of a fiddle with the back wheel, and it may be necessary to partly unscrew the hub.

3. You won't get the tube out unless it is well deflated. Carefully insert a lever to get the tyre wall off the rim, and then work the rim off all the way round one side using two levers.

4. Pull the tube out of the tyre. The next thing is to find the puncture. Inflate the tube, and then slowly pass it close to your ear and cheek. You should hear or feel the leak and be able to locate it. If this fails, you can try submerging the tube in a puddle and watch for tell-tale bubbles.

5. When you've found the puncture, keep a finger on it so you don't lose it. Roughen the surrounding area with the 'roughener' provided in your repair kit, and then cover the area with a patch-sized blob of glue. Now leave the glue to set for at least two minutes.

6. To find out what caused the puncture, run your fingers round the inside of the tyre; the probable cause is a thorn which is still in the tyre. Remove it carefully.

7. The glue should now be set enough to put on the patch which should bond straight to the tube. If it seems OK, partly inflate the tube, which makes things easier when getting the tyre back onto the rim.

8. Reassemble the wheel and put it back on the bike. Connecting the brake cable first ensures the wheel is centred by a pull on the brake lever before you tighten the quick release hub; it also ensures you don't ride off with the brake undone. Now inflate the tyre fully.

Mending the tube is usually a quick operation.

SAFETY OFFROAD

The first rule of offroad touring is to allow enough time. Getting caught by nightfall is foolhardy and potentially dangerous, particularly if the ride ends in an on-road section and you have no lights. So before you leave, work out how much time to allow, and be pessimistic. Your speed will depend on your skill, level of fitness, and the riding conditions.

Tackling a route after heavy rain in midwinter may take three times as long as the same route in dry summer weather. Riding along a disused railway line will be fast and easy; riding up and down big hills can be exceptionally demanding, and the difference in speed between a good and not so good rider will be much greater.

Riding in a group should ensure some degree of safety, but groups which are much bigger than three riders bring their own problems. They can put an unacceptable load on other people's enjoyment of the environment; walkers and horseriders were there first, and while they can cope with small groups of bike riders, it's no fun for them when a dozen or so Tour de France lookalikes blast through their favourite countryside. By contrast riding alone has much to recommend it; you cause minimum upset to others, and also don't have to worry about keeping up with the fastest member of the group, while the slowest rider doesn't have to worry about keeping up with you.

Whether you ride alone or in a small group, before leaving the golden rule is *tell someone:*

- When you're going.
- When you expect to be back.
- Give them some idea of your route.

It doesn't happen often, but riders do occasionally fall off and knock themselves out or break a few bones in the middle of nowhere; if that happened to you, it would be nice to know that someone would come looking for you, and that they'd be able to locate you before too long.

A First Aid kit is only of value if someone knows how to use it, and even then the constric-

Don't 'race' unless it's official.

tions of space and weight on a bike will make its application limited; some bandages and plasters will be enough to deal with minor cuts and abrasions, or possibly support a fracture. In most cases injuries from falls are fairly minor, and you can keep on riding; in more serious cases it will probably be a case of getting help ASAP, while caring for the injured rider:

- If two crash, help the worst injured first.
- If a rider is unconscious, don't leave him on his back. Use the First Aid 'recovery position' if you know how, and cover him with a coat if possible. If a rider is unconscious and not breathing, give the kiss of life if you know how.
- Staunch any bleeding by applying a pad or hand pressure; if bleeding is in an arm or leg, raise the injured limb unless broken.
- Don't move the rider if he seems to be paralysed, unless in immediate danger.
- Don't give the rider anything to eat, drink or smoke.
- Don't leave the injured rider alone.

If you ride regularly it's well worth attending a full length course to get a First Aid certificate which is valid for three years. These are run all round the UK by organizations such as the British Red Cross Society, whose phone number can be found in the local telephone directory.

The South Downs

The South Downs of Sussex are one of the prime offroad cycling areas in the UK. The landscape that they straddle also offers some wonderfully quiet country lanes, enabling the cyclist mostly to avoid the horrors of busy roads and to make the most of the huge choice of pubs on the routes that he follows. Most of these routes are based around the long-distance South Downs Way, ranging from west to east from the Hampshire border through Sussex.

Ride 1:   Chichester to Petworth

Ride 2:   Stoughton and Harting Downs

Ride 3:   From Petworth to Bramber

Ride 4:   Around Haywards Heath

Ride 5:   The South Downs Way

Ride 6:   From Queen Elizabeth Country Park

Ride 7:   Kingley Vale and Stansted

Ride 8:   Goodwood and the Downs

Ride 9:   Selhurst Park and the Downs

Ride 10: Bignor Hill and the Downs

Ride 11: River Arun Ride

Ride 12: Chanctonbury and Cissbury Rings

Ride 13: Bramber Castle and the Downs

Ride 14: Bramber Castle and the Downs Link

Ride 15: Bramber Castle to Wolstonbury Hill

Ride 16: Ditchling Beacon and the Downs

Ride 17: Firle Beacon and the Downs

Ride 18: Alfriston and the Downs

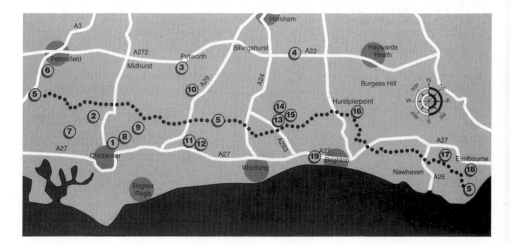

From Chichester to Petworth

Mainly On-Road

RIDE 1

Area: The western end of the South Downs, going as far west as the Hampshire border.

OS Map: Landranger 197 Chichester and the Downs.

Route:
Chichester (GR:860047)
Bosham (GR:803038)
South Harting (GR:776197)
Midhurst (GR:887214)
Petworth (GR:978218)
Bignor Hill (GR:973130)
Walberton (GR:970060)
Chichester (GR:860047)

Nearest BR Station: Chichester.

Approx Length: 70 miles (113km).

Time: Allow at least 7 hours in the saddle, plus time to stop and look around, visit pubs, explore towns and villages.

Rating: Moderate. Virtually the whole length of this ride is on-road, but there are plenty of hills and it is a good distance which makes it a very full day out. Most of the roads are comparatively quiet and car-free, and much of the distance is really delightful cycling.

This ride – and its two companions (Rides 3 and 4) – is based on the 200 mile (322 km) Cycling Round West Sussex route, published by West Sussex County Council. These rides break down the route into three sections which can each be tackled in a day, though the distances are quite long and with so much to see and do you may prefer to break each section into a two-day trip with an overnight stop. These three rides also attempt to avoid some of the busier road sections of the official route, so cars should not be too much of a problem. Despite being virtually all on-road, they make for delightful riding on a fine day.

1. Chichester, being the 'capital' of West Sussex, is the obvious place to start this ride and has the benefit of a main line railway station. You can of course start the ride where you wish, with Midhurst and Petworth being convenient towns along the way. Chichester itself has plenty of car parking, and some of the car parks on the outskirts of the town are free on Saturdays as well as Sundays. The Cathedral dominates the city, and makes a good place to start from.

2. Head west along West Street from the Cathedral, crossing straight over at the roundabout onto the brick paved road which continues westwards. The brick paving and traffic islands along this stretch are Chichester's very expensive and almost totally unsuccessful attempt to 'calm' the traffic, and represent a perfect example of a traffic planner who has shown minimal interest in the needs of cyclists. Keep straight on across the railway line and ride through the bridge under the A27, joining the A259 close to Chichester.

3. The A259 is possibly the busiest road section on this ride, though thankfully it doesn't last for long. Look out for the sign for the Roman Palace at Fishbourne on the north side – if you are interested in antiquities it has a small museum and a fine display of mosaic floors, plus a cyclist-friendly small cafe, which will reward at least a two-hour visit. Ride on along the A259, if necessary using the south side pavement which is bike friendly

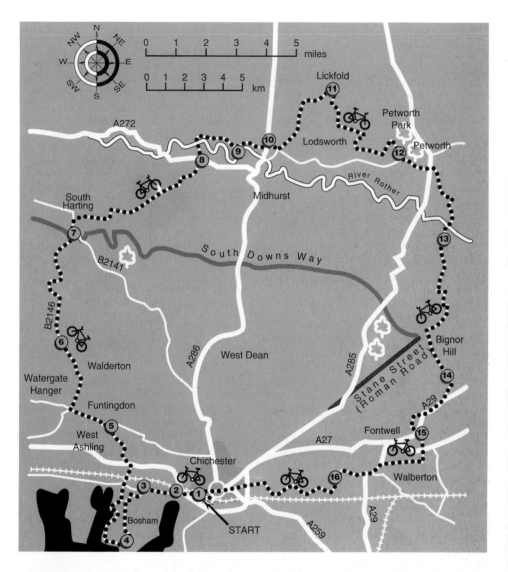

here. Look out for the bike/motorbike shop on the north side which is run in delightful fashion by a family of true two-wheel enthusiasts, passing The Black Boy pub and then turning left off the main road just past Brinkman's Nursery.

This quiet lane leads south and west towards Bosham, turning left into Walton Lane and right past the entrance to Rectory Farm. Take the next left into Taylor's Lane, and follow this long road southwards through open farmland, finally reaching the entrance to Bosham Hoe, an exclusive hideaway development of large houses on the shores of Chichester Harbour; here the road swings west along Smuggler's Lane. On the corner where it swings north again, look out for the footpath pointing south from a patch of gravel –

Riding into South Harting the Coach and Horses awaits your pleasure.

it's worth the short walk down this track to enjoy the view across to Itchenor.

4. The road continues to follow the side of the Bosham peninsula, offering fine views over to the village which can be seen on the other side of the water. Ride on round to Bosham; its quaint character tends to attract an invasion of cars at weekends and much of the time in high season. The crowded pub here is the Anchor Bleu – note that the road round the foreshore is covered at high tide, and there is no finer sight than a car which gets 'drowned'.

5. From Bosham follow the road up past the Millstream Hotel, turning left to re-cross the A259, taking the B2146 to West Ashling. Turn left in the village, and then turn right by the large duckpond, following a narrow lane northwards by the side of a stream into Funtington; here there is a reasonable pub and a particularly excellent farm shop with pick-your-own fields in season.

Turn right, to continue on the B2146 sign-posted to Petersfield. A steady uphill takes you to the top of a hill from where there is a fine view over to the Racton Monument, a tower folly on the opposite hillside; at the bottom of the hill, watch out for traffic crossing on the B2147.

6. The B2147 meanders northwards through a very pleasant valley landscape, with pubs in quiet settings at Walderton or West Marden (though last time I went the latter was neither bike nor child friendly). Between Walderton and West Marden look out for the huge classical house on the hillside to the right; amazingly this was built in the 1980s, replacing a house that was inadvertently burnt to the ground by billeted servicemen during World War II.

7. The only bad news along this stretch is that the road is a slight but steady uphill for much of the way. It passes the National Trust house at Uppark which has been totally restored after a much more recent fire; it was due to be fully open to the public from 1995.

Past Uppark the B2146 crosses the South Downs Way, going steeply downhill into South Harting. Ride through the village – which is a pretty place with a good pub on the way in – and bear right on the minor road signposted for East Harting and Elsted, where you will find another suitable pub. This stretch of road prvides a magnificent view of the downs. Then bear north-east at Lower Elsted, where there is yet another agreeable pub just as you start to go down the hill, passing through dense woods en route for Iping Common; here an optional stretch of bridleway slices off a corner of the road, and is easily ridden even in fairly wet weater.

8. This brings you out to a car park opposite the nature reserve at Stedham Common, after which the road comes to the main A272. Turn right and left to cross straight over here, and follow the narrow road ahead through the hamlet of Iping crossing the River Rother over a narrow bridge.

Take the next right turn which is rather vaguely signposted to Hammerwood, and follow the narrow, one-car's-width lane which can be so covered with mud and muck that it's rather like going offroad. This is an-up-and-down ride through lovely unspoilt countryside, eventually bearing south-east to come to the hamlet of Woolbeding.

9. Woolbeding is an extraordinary place, a hamlet consisting of about half-a-dozen huge and very imposing mansions, and not much besides. Turn right to take a look at the churchyard which is particularly attractive, situated right next to a very fine mansion with beautiful grounds; this is Simon Sainsbury's weekend 'cottage'!

From Woolbeding the road continues east along a ridge, with fine views over the beautiful valley of the River Rother and passing several most desirable residences along the way. The route continues until it crosses the A286 towards Easebourne, though you may like to divert into Midhurst which is an agreeable country town with a small but fine ruined castle on the banks of the Rother close to Cowdray Park.

10. Rejoin the route at Easebourne, and immediately turn left onto an unsignposted lane opposite the large church on the sharp right-hand bend in the A272. This leads steadily uphill past a few shops, a couple of pubs and some very pleasant-looking Georgian houses, heading out into open country and from there up, up and up to the top of Bexleyhill Common; from where it's a very fast downhill all the way to Lickfold, with its agreeable green and the expensive-looking Lickfold Arms, where you can stop for a drink.

11. From Lickfold follow the road due south past Lodsworth Common, bearing left at the top of Leggatt Hill on the road for River and Upperton. This meanders along the valley side with a fair few ups and downs, eventually dropping downhill through Upperton, passing alongside the huge grounds of Petworth Park and coming downhill to the main A272 at Tillington. Here there is a very fine church with an unusual four-cornered spire, and the pub right opposite.

12. Turn left along the A272 for the short ride into Petworth; if you don't like the main road after so much time spent on quiet lanes, you can safely ride on the pavement here. At the roundabout turn left uphill into Petworth, which brings you up to the gates of Petworth House (NT) with its deer park.

13. After a good look round Petworth – particularly interesting if you like nosing about in antique shops – follow the minor road which heads due south towards Haslingbourne, turning left (east) towards Fittleworth and right at the next turn to continue southwards towards the downs which can be seen ahead. Crossing the River Rother at Shopham Bridge, this narrow lane takes you through delightful countryside to Sutton, emerging by the pub on the corner. Turn left and follow the signposts to Bignor with its up and down hills and Roman villa, joining the dead-end road which continues south and zig-zags steeply up the side of the down to the car park at the top of Bignor Hill on the South Downs Way.

14. From Bignor Hill, follow the large signpost in the direction of Slindon on the short bridleway section that connects with the next road. The bridleway goes south past Great Bottom and Stammers on a good track, heading quickly downhill to join the tarmac lane at Stammers on the south side of the down. Follow the road straight ahead here, keeping south to join the A29 by the side of Rewell Hill. This is often a very busy stretch of road, but thankfully you don't have to ride too far. Follow the road until it bears right uphill, turning off for Slindon by the gatehouse at the top of the hill – be very careful of speeding traffic here as there is a dual carriageway leading up from the other side.

15. Follow the quiet road ahead uphill and into Slindon, bearing left past the pub to continue south. Cross the A29 with care, going straight ahead to cross the A27 with even greater care; you can either push your bike across, or take the right turn as indicated. This brings you south as far as Walberton, from where it's a steady ride westwards back to Chichester. The country is very flat and open here, and with a prevailing south-westerly wind it can be heavy going. The scenery is not of the best, but there are some pleasant surprises along the way.

16. The traffic is fairly light as you head via Aldingbourne, along the perimeter of the old Battle of Britain airfield at Tangmere, to Oving with its neat thatched pub which would make a suitable place for a final countryside drink. Follow the road on to Shopwyke, following the road straight across the A27 and into the centre of Chichester, then push your bike up the main pedestrian precinct to get back to the Cathedral after a long, but very pleasant ride.

The fine church at Upperton near Petworth.

Places To Visit:
Chichester Cathedral
(tel: 01243 782595);
Fishbourne Roman Palace
(tel: 01243 785859);
Uppark NT* (tel: 01730 725317);
Petworth House and Park NT*
(tel: 01798 42207).
*National Trust

Top Pubs:
Anchor Bleu in Bosham;
The Ship at South Harting;
The Lickfold Arms at Lickfold;
The Gribble at Oving.

Stoughton and Harting Downs

Mainly Offroad

Area: The western end of the South Downs, between Petersfield and Chichester.

OS Map: Landranger 197 Chichester and the Downs.

Route:
Harting Downs CP/South Downs Way (GR:793183)
Beacon Hill/SDW (GR:809183)
Hooksway (GR:815162)
North Marden (GR:808161)
East Marden (GR:807145)
Stoughton (GR:802115)
Walderton (GR:790107)
Telegraph Hill (GR:783150)
Harting Downs CP/South Downs Way (GR:793183)

Nearest BR Stations: Southbourne/ Bosham/Chichester.

Approx Length: 15 miles (24km).

Time: Allow 3 hours.

Rating: Moderate, with some steady ups and downs along the SDW.

There is a large, free car park at the top of Harting Downs, on the east side of the B2141, just over a mile to the south-east of South Harting. It's a good place to start, but take care on fine weekends as the car park draws a lot of walkers to the immediate area of Harting Downs.

1. Ride eastwards along the SDW, with fine views to the north over East Harting. Some way on the track leads steeply downhill to the old signpost at Crossdykes. This is at the foot of Beacon Hill which is ultra steep, so take the alternative SDW route which bears right along the southern side of the hill, turning sharp left to the north to rejoin the SDW just before reaching Telegraph House. Continue to follow the SDW downhill along the side of woods, eventually coming to a gate by a main crossing track just above Buriton Farm.

2. Turn right along this hard track, heading downhill through the valley and passing Buriton Farm on the left. The track climbs a little – it can be very muddy here – before levelling out. If you want to visit The Royal Oak at Hooksway, look out for the bridleway signpost pointing straight across the field on the left and follow the track towards the pub; the main track climbs up the hillside, emerging on the road a short way above The Royal Oak.

3. From The Royal Oak turn right steeply uphill on the access road that leads to the B2141. Turn right onto this road, and then after a short distance of easy freewheeling downhill take the first left signposted to North Marden; this is a tiny hamlet with a very pretty small church. From here a narrow country lane leads downhill to East Marden with its splendid old water well; here you bear right for Stoughton, through Wildham Wood and on past the car park at Lamdown Hill (an alternative good place to start this ride – GR:814126).

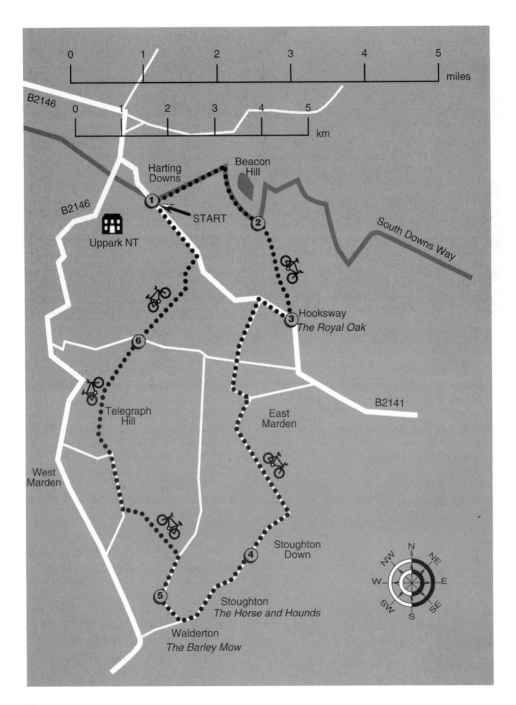

Stop for a rest at the pretty Hamlet of East Marden.

4. Ride on through Stoughton in the shadow of Kingley Vale, where you have the option of stopping at the pub. There is also a pleasant pub at the next village, which is Walderton; however, a short distance before you get there the route itself actually turns right up a lane signposted to Upper Marden.

Follow this lane round to the right, ignoring the first turn to the left, and looking out for a bridleway crossroads. Turn left here, following the bridleway uphill into the trees of Haslett Copse, and then bearing left to follow the bridleway track away from two isolated houses.

5. Turn right along the next lane, and follow it northwards past Locksash Farm on the corner. Follow the road round to the left here, and then as the road drops downhill look out for the bridleway turning on the right; follow this track, which continues northwards.

Cross beneath the overhead powerlines, following the bridleway along the edge of a field and past the house on Telegraph Hill. As you start to go downhill along the track past Bevis's Thumb you can clearly see Uppark (National Trust stately home) on the opposite hillside.

6. Cross straight over the next lane, and follow the bridleway along the side of fields going north-east towards the B2141. Just before the road you pass close by a splendid Uppark gatehouse, then turn left along the B2141. A mile or so further on, turn right onto the SDW at Harting Downs.

> ***Places To Visit:***
> Uppark NT (Tel: 01730 825317).
>
> ***Top Pubs:***
> The Royal Oak at Hooksway;
> The Barley Mow at Walderton;
> The Horse and Hounds at Stoughton.

From Petworth to Bramber

Mainly On-Road
Some Offroad

Area: Eastwards of Petworth along the north side of the South Downs.

OS Map: Landranger 197/198 Chichester and the Downs/Brighton and the Downs.

Route:
Petworth (GR:978218)
Wisborough Green (GR:052259)
Southwater/Downs Link (GR:160260)
Bramber (GR:185106)
Storrington (GR:086143)
Amberley (GR:027132)
Petworth (GR:978218)

Nearest BR Stations:
Billingshurst/Amberley.

Approx Length: 60 miles (96.5km).

Time: Allow at least 6 hours in the saddle, plus time to stop and look around, visit pubs, explore the towns en route, and so on.

Rating: Moderate. Most of this ride is on-road, but as it is a good distance it makes a full day out. There are several optional offroad sections which will increase both time and difficulty; after extended wet weather the Downs Link can have a surprising amount of mud and big puddles.

This route uses the central part of the 200 mile (322km) Cycling Round West Sussex *route, published by West Sussex County Council. The distance is quite long and there is plenty to see, which makes it a good ride for a full day out.*

Unlike the two other rides based on this West Sussex route, there is a long offroad section using the Downs Link, though as long as the track is dry this is easy riding. For those who want to avoid the 'A' roads connecting the part of the route between Bramber and Storrington, there is also the possibility of joining the South Downs Way between Steyning and Amberley. This could add at least an hour to the time taken and make the whole circuit considerably more tiring, but has the very real benefit of getting well away from cars.

1. From the centre of Petworth, head north on the A283, passing the long wall of Petworth Park on the left and the main car park and entrance to Petworth House (NT). Look out for the signpost to Balls Cross which forks off to the right, turning off at Hampers Green.

2. At first this road seems rather uninspiring, but it soon improves, with relatively little traffic and gentle ups and downs which make for excellent fast riding through mainly woodland and open fields. Balls Cross is the first settlement of any size, and features some very comfortable houses as well as a pub; from here, fork right to Kirdford which has a very pretty 'square' opposite the church and two pleasant-looking pubs. Take the left fork here, following the road round to Wisborough Green; both church and pub are situated close to the huge green, which frequently hosts cricket matches in the summer.

3. Cross straight over at the green, following the quiet back road in a north-east direction to join the B2133 at Newpound Common. Here the official West Sussex route links up with the

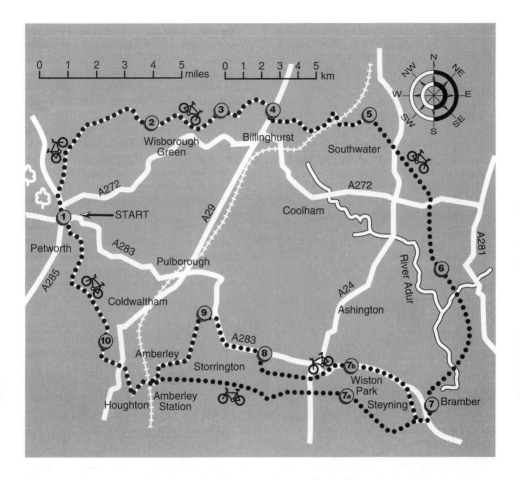

A272 and crosses the River Arun on the out-skirts of Billingshurst. An alternative recommended short cut in dry weather is to follow the bridleway sign that points straight ahead, following the track past Raplands Farm and across the Wey and Arun Canal by a lock in surroundings that are pretty, though marred by electricity pylons marching across the land. A second bridge leads over the nearby River Arun by the side of some interesting sluice gates, and from here the track goes up to the extremely smart Rowner Farm – though the way up can be very muddy – and out onto a lane.

4. Follow this lane to the north of Billingshurst, moving onto OS198 as you join the A29. This dead straight section of road was part of the Roman Stane Street; for cyclists its straightness means that cars approach very fast, and great care needs to be taken when crossing to the other side and heading southwards. For those interested in antiques or old paintings, look out for Sotheby's at Summers Place by the side of the road here – if an auction is on view it is well worth stopping to visit.

5. A short way past Sotheby's, take the first turning on the left for a resumption of quiet, countryside cycling. Follow the road on to Barns Green with its pub, and from there to Two Mile Ash where a road bridge crosses the Downs Link old railway, with a convenient pub on the far side of the line.

6. A track leads down onto the line on the west side, and from here you can follow the Downs Link offroad virtually all the way to Bramber (see Ride 19 for full Downs Link details). Be warned that while the Downs Link is an enjoyable ride in dry weather, some sections have very poor drainage and become extremely wet and muddy after extended rain.

7. The next section of the route leads from Bramber Castle westwards. The official West Sussex route sends riders along the busy A283 most of the way to Storrington and beyond – for sure this is the quickest way of getting there with fine views of the north side of the Downs, but with fast traffic buzzing by it's not the most pleasant way to pedal almost 10 miles on-road. There are two recommended alternatives:

7a. If it is dry and you still have plenty of energy, it's an easy matter to join the South Downs Way above Steyning and follow it westwards all the way to Amberley; this cuts out this entire road section, and navigation is quite straightforward. This is the way I would recommend; the only real disadvantage is that you miss some pleasant riding between Greatham and Amberley.

7b. If you prefer to stay on low ground, Steyning is a pleasant small town to ride

The Downs Link is extremely popular with leisure cyclists.

through, and this cuts off a good chunk of the A283. From here, the map shows that a route through Wiston Park might be possible; however the road is unfortunately not a right of way for bikes, and the path which puts you back on the A283 is only footpath.

From Washington things improve, with a bridleway leading westwards. Turn into Washington village, which is surprisingly pleasant despite its proximity to the A24, following School Lane past the pub and uphill towards the church. From here the bridleway bridge leads over the A24, with bridleways turning right to go back down to the road, left to go up to the top of the downs, or going straight ahead across fields to the splendidly isolated church at Sullington. The latter track can be pleasant in dry weather (though well used by horses), with fine views of the downs in rural surroundings. It brings you back to the A283 on the outskirts of Storrington.

8. Once back on the A283, follow this track onto OS197 and down into Storrington, a pleasant enough small town though rather besieged by motor traffic. Keep west along the A283 – look out for the cycle shop on the west side of the town – following the road towards Pulborough with Parham House and its deer park on the left. Once again, there is the potential for a cycle-friendly route across Parham Park here, but sadly it is only recognized as footpath.

9. Past Northpark Wood, take the first turning left off the A283 signposted to Greatham. At last you are back onto pleasant, quiet roads, skirting the side of the huge Parham estate with little traffic and very few buildings. Take the left turn signposted to Rackham, passing the west entrance to Parham and then turning

towards Amberley with two pubs along the way, and Amberley Castle (a 'Country House Hotel') on the outskirts of the village. Here you join the B2139 for a short way, meeting up with the South Downs Way, where the new SDW bridges lead across the railway line and the River Arun, joining a lane south of Bury.

10. Ride through Bury and cross the A29, taking the lane to West Burton and then following the signs to Bignorpark. This is extremely pleasant riding, probably the best of the whole route. Gentle ups and downs lead through beautiful wooded countryside, with the imposing mass of the downs gradually left behind. Past Bignorpark take the turning signposted to Petworth, crossing the River Rother at Shopham Bridge and continuing northwards to Petworth, a town which has countless teashops and pubs just waiting for you!

Places To Visit:
Petworth House and Park NT (tel: 01798 42207);
Sotheby's at Billingshurst (tel: 01403 783933);
Parham House and Park (tel: 01903 744888);
Amberley Chalk Pits Museum (tel: 01798 831370).

Top Pubs:
The Half Moon at Kirdford;
The Three Crowns and The Bat & Ball at Wisborough Green;
The Frankland Arms at Washington;
The Bridge Inn at Amberley.

Around Haywards Heath

Mainly On-Road

Area: Along the north side of the South Downs around Haywards Heath.

OS Map: Landranger 198/187 Brighton & the Downs/Dorking, Reigate & Crawley.

Route:
Cowfold (GR:213227)
Warninglid (GR:250261)
Staplefield (GR:280282)
Balcombe (GR:310308)
Ardingly (GR:348294)
Horsted Keynes Station (GR:371293)
Scayne's Hill (GR:369232)
Westmeston (GR:338137)
Hurstpierpoint (GR:280165)
Wineham (GR:236200)
Cowfold (GR:213227)

Nearest BR Stations:
Hassocks/Balcombe.

Approx Length: 55 miles (88km).

Time: Allow 5 hours in the saddle, plus time to stop and look around, visit pubs, explore the towns en route, and so on.

Rating: Moderate. All of this ride is on-road, with a few optional offroad sections. It is easy riding, with plenty to see.

This ride uses the eastern part of the 200 mile (322km) Cycling Round West Sussex route and stays firmly on-road, although plenty of offroad diversions are possible. It visits delightful country along the way, despite being close to major conurbations, and most of the route is reasonably traffic-free, particularly if when you tackle it you avoid busy summer weekends when cars are out for their regular 'wiffle'.

There are a number of convenient points to start the ride along the route. I chose the village of Cowfold, on the A272 just three miles east of the Downs Link, which has the advantage of a free car park, and a village green with loos, pub and a few shops. The route is also well served by trains, Hassocks and Balcombe being the nearest stations.

1. From Cowfold, ride along the A272 a short way eastwards, taking the first turn on the left signposted Warninglid. Almost immediately you are in a different world, away from the main road with scarcely a car to be seen during a fine day in mid-March. The countryside along the way is immaculate, and so are the houses – there are some very comfortable residences hereabouts.

Just past the first pub along the road look out for the exceptionally fine house at Warninglid; cross straight over the B2115 and follow the road on ahead with easy ups and downs until you come to the crossroads by a pond at Slaugham Common. Turn right here, following the signpost for Staplefield.

2. Ride on through Slaugham – it has a pleasant-looking pub, though for my taste set in somewhat 'bijou' surroundings, opposite the church – and on under the A23, which surprisingly doesn't impinge on the countryside; the bridge has very fine old arches and is a world away from those modern concrete motorway monstrosities.

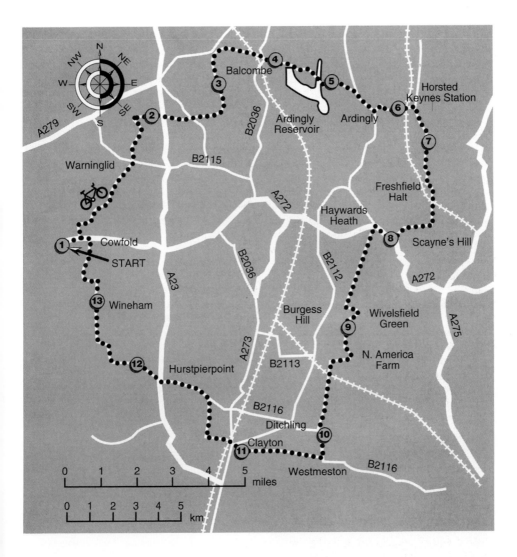

The next stop is Staplefield, where you ride along by the side of the huge green, crossing straight over the B2114. If you want to divert to Nymans Gardens (NT), these are just over a mile away along the B2114 to the north-west. Ride on past the imposing Tyes Place where the road bears round to the north on an uphill that takes you past The Rifleman pub.

3. From here on, despite the steady uphill, it is really delightful riding with fine views over open country, and with luck scarcely a car to be seen. The road continues due north, reaching the B2110 by Brantridge Park close to an impressive water tower – the Victorians really knew how to build these monuments to their civic pride.

4. Turn right here, following the minor road eastwards to Balcombe, sweeping downhill through woodland and across the railway line, before coming to the B2036 on the outskirts of Balcombe, which is a sizeable village. Turn right past the church here, almost immediately forking left opposite the pub to follow the lane signposted for Ardingly.

On the outskirts of Balcombe go steady, because the next left turn for Ardingly is easily overshot; join a narrow lane which heads steeply downhill towards Ardingly reservoir, with a magnificent series of zig-zags and glimpses of the reservoir opening out below. The road drops to cross the northern leg of the reservoir in a very pretty setting; if you fancy some offroading there is a signposted bridleway which runs round the reservoir shoreline, although it is probably best avoided at weekends when it is popular with walkers.

5. What goes down must go up, and after the first drop to cross the reservoir there is a steady climb to the top of West Hill. At the top take the next right turn above Lullings, which leads to a superb downhill to cross the north-east arm of the reservoir. Huge speeds are attainable if you dare!

The famous Bluebell Railway is on the route of this ride.

6. From here, it's a steady plug uphill to the outskirts of Ardingly, following the signs through this oversized village to join the B2028. The gardens of Wakehurst Place (NT) are about two miles (3.2km) to the north here. The main route continues south along the B2028, leading out into open country, and then turning off to the left onto a lane signposted to Highbrook. Follow this downhill, turning right at the bottom towards Horsted Keynes, following the side of the old disused railway (another potentially wonderful cycletrack/walkway) through to the headquarters of the famous Bluebell Railway at Horsted Keynes station, which is a must for steam buffs.

7. From here, follow the road south past Horsted Keynes itself, riding through quiet countryside, following the signs to Scaynes Hill, and crossing the Bluebell Railway just south of Freshfield Halt. A short way on, the road crosses the River Ouse by a pub in a setting that is well worth a stop; after this you reach Scayne's Hill, where you abruptly hit the A272, the first really busy road so far encountered on this ride.

8. Turn west along the A272 signposted to Hayward's Heath; for an 'A' road it isn't too bad, with plenty of width to allow co-existence of cycles and motor traffic. After less than a mile you can take the first left turning off it, following an unsignposted lane that leads due south to Wivelsfield. In no time at all you are back to the best of British country lane riding, crossing the Sussex Border Path and passing the impressive Townings Place situated on top of the hill, with views of the South Downs coming into sight ahead.

9. Wivelsfield is a peaceful sort of place; take a left turn here, and then a right on the outskirts of Wivelsfield Green signposted for Ditchling. Fork left on the narrow lane which leads uphill through West Wood, and ride down to the next road junction by the strangely named North America Farm. Turn right, and

All aboard the Bluebell Railway, if you've got time.

stretch of 'A' road is pretty unpleasant, so take care. Once you have turned off, however, do stop to look at the extraordinary house that has been built into the railway arch.

12. Follow the lane west beneath Wolstonbury Hill, bearing round to the north to leave the downs and join the B2116 on the outskirts of Hassocks. From here follow the road through Hurstpierpoint – which has some memorable Regency buildings – then ride on to join the A23 at Aldbourne. Turn right at the traffic lights opposite the pub here, and almost immediately turn left off the A23, to continue along the B2116 in the direction of High Cross.

13. About a mile further on, take the next right turn for Wineham, heading north to cross the River Adur. Ride on through Wineham, passing a pub. Take the next left turn to Kent Street if you wish to return to Cowfold, or ride straight on north if you're heading for Warninglid.

then next left here, still heading south towards the downs; you cross the railway line by Blackbreak Wood, and reach the B2116 on the outskirts of Ditchling.

10. Turn left here, following the B2116 south past Westmeston Place to the hamlet of Westmeston. Turn right by the church and phone box, joining the narrow lane which follows the foot of the South Downs due west all the way to Clayton. This is a lovely ride, but if you fancy a diversion to the top of the downs and the weather is dry, you can follow the bridleway which leads straight ahead, riding along the top to Ditchling Beacon, and descending on the ultra steep road (part of the London-Brighton cycle route) that leads back down to Wick Farm.

11. Follow the road through Clayton, looking back to see the twin Jack and Jill windmills near the top of the down. Turn right along the A273, almost immediately turning left onto a lane by the pub on the corner. This short

---

Places To Visit:
Nymans Gardens NT
(tel: 01444 400321);
Wakehurst Place NT
(tel: 01444 892701);
Bluebell Line Railway
(tel: 01825 722370).

Top Pubs:
The Rifleman at Staplehurst;
The Sloop at Scayne's Hill;
The White House at Hurstpierpoint.

The South Downs Way

Mainly Offroad

Area: The South Downs of Sussex, between Petworth and Eastbourne.

OS Maps: Landrangers 197/198/199 Chichester and the Downs/Brighton and the Downs/Eastbourne, Hastings and surrounding area.

Route:
Queen Elizabeth Country Park (GR:718185)
CP south of Buriton (GR:733198)
South Harting (GR:780186)
Cocking (GR:876167)
Bignor Hill (GR:982131)
Houghton (GR:016118)
Rackham Hill (GR:053126)
Washington (GR:119120)
Steyning Bowl (GR:162094)
Botolphs/River Adur/Downs Link (GR:194093)

Tottington Barn/YHA (GR:220105)
Devil's Dyke (GR:260108)
Saddlescombe (GR:273116)
Ditchling Beacon (GR:332131)
Kingston near Lewes (GR:383079)
Rodmell (GR:060420)
Firle Beacon (GR:486059)
Alfriston (GR:520030)
Jevington (GR:562013)
Eastbourne (GR:596982)

Nearest BR Stations: Petersfield/ Amberley/Southease/Eastbourne.

Approx Length: 80 miles (129km).

Time: One day is very hard; two days is moderate; three days is getting easy.

Rating: Hard/Moderate. There are a lot of ups and downs, which can be dispiriting. Some sections can feature mud, but mostly it is very good riding.

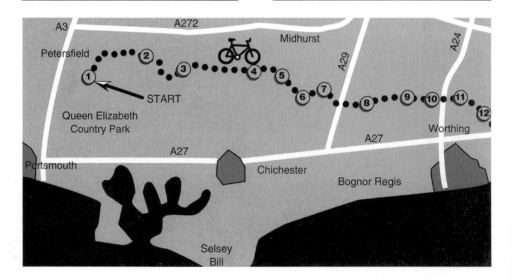

The South Downs Way traverses the South Downs. Apart from being a very popular long-distance footpath, the route is also non-stop bridleway virtually all the way, with the principal exception of the Seven Sisters coastal loop which is footpath only, whilst the bridleway follows the downs inland. An extension has recently been introduced which connects the SDW to Winchester, adding some 25 miles (40km); apart from being outside the scope of this book by plunging into Hampshire, this part of the route offers less scope for bikers since it ceases to be the virtual non-stop bridleway of the remaining 80 miles (129km).

If the weather is kind the views are good, and with a few noisy exceptions the route is infrequently crossed by roads. Its character changes along its length: the first half of the route from the Sussex/Hampshire border as far as Steyning is less touched by modern farming, with woodland sections, plenty of wildlife, and the prettiest villages; the second half is more open grassland, and can be bleak when riding in the face of lashing rain or a strong headwind. Since the prevailing wind is normally from the west and the best railway connections are at the Eastbourne

end, we prefer to ride this route from west to east - but there is nothing to stop you doing it the other way.

The SDW is an up-and-down route, following the high chalk ridges of the downs and dipping in and out of valleys, so be prepared for a lot of hill climbing and some exciting descents. Most of the route is easily followed, with the traditional acorn LDP sign showing the way, but there are one or two places where it is easy to go at full speed past an important turn-off, so run your eye over the OS map before tackling each section.

1. You can start from the Queen Elizabeth Country Park, on the A3 south of Petersfield; this is all right if you are arriving by car, but it isn't a bike-friendly place to get to if you're riding from Petersfield BR station. It can also be confusing finding the correct route through the thick woods of War Down to join the start of the SDW. The alternative is to make for the small village of Buriton, just over two miles due south of Petersfield. Take the road that goes south beneath the railway line to Rowlands Castle, and you'll find a car park on the right at the foot of War Down. This is directly opposite a dead-end lane which passes Coulters Dean Farm and leads

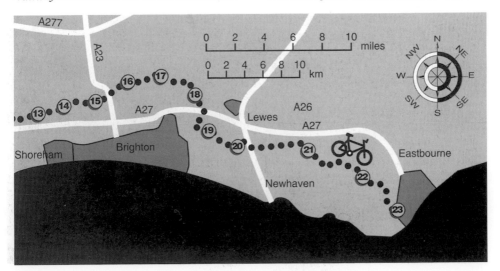

via a road to Sunwood Farm on the Hampshire/Sussex border; this was the original official start/end of the SDW before the addition of the extra leg to Winchester.

2. The South Downs Way acorn signs point out the way along chalk tracks, with some severely muddy stretches in wet weather towards Harting Downs. The first village down the hillside to the left is South Harting, once the home of both Alexander Pope and Anthony Trollope. A short way on, you emerge at the top of Harting Downs by a car park, to experience the first of many fine views the South Downs Way offers. To the south-west the views extend across Chichester Harbour to the Isle of Wight; to the south-east across the city of Chichester. Here the route follows a fine grassy trail along the top of the down, giving fast and easy riding.

3. Down a hill the ancient signpost at Cross Dykes is the next landmark, with the much smaller South Downs Way signpost giving three options: a 'bike impossible' climb straight up Beacon Hill with its ancient Iron Age hill fort on top; the more realistic climb which skirts the hill with a sharp left turn at the top; or straight on where the bridleway goes past Telegraph House and on to The Royal Oak at Hooksway.

4. The SDW drops downhill towards Buriton Farm; then a long climb to the top of Linch Down takes you past The Devil's Jumps, five Bronze Age round barrows. The route passes through ancient woodland, bearing round the back of Monkton House. Linch Down is heavily wooded but offers good riding, passing by Linchball and Westdean Woods which afford excellent protection against wind and rain. Agricultural land reasserts itself once again, and a fine view opens to the east as you thwack down towards the A286 on a fast but bumpy track. Cocking village is about half a mile to the north with its church, duckpond, and choice of two public houses.

5. A good climb starts by Hill Barn Farm (fill up at the water tap opposite), the track heading steeply uphill past Manorfarm Down and Heyshott Down. Along the top of the down the views are shrouded by dense woodland, as the route passes the village of Heyshott to the north and some way on Grafham, where the Victorian free trader Richard Cobden lived. Off to the right is the top of Littleton Down. Crown Tegleaze at at 255m is the highest point of the Sussex Downs.

6. Another long downhill brings your overheated brakes to the A285 Petworth/Chichester road by the side of Littleton Farm. A stark white chalk track wends its way up to the top of Burton Down, homing in towards the radio masts. As you grind upwards, rest assured that it's a classic descent in the other direction! The SDW passes to the south of the masts along a narrow and sometimes very muddy track, crossing National Trust land. Soon you ride through the car park at Bignor Hill, from where you may glimpse the thatched buildings that protect the Roman Mosaics of Bignor on the plain below. Take it easy as this part of the route is usually well filled with Sunday afternoon walkers in summertime, congregating at the Bignor Post which shows the way along Stane Street, built by the Romans to connect London Bridge with Chichester's East Gate in the first century AD.

Gates, gates and more gates on the South Down Way.

7. The SDW follows a hard chalk track to the east along the top of the down, with fine views southwards and ahead as far as Chanctonbury Ring. Pass the mounting block known as Toby's Stone, a memorial to Toby Wentworth-Fitzwilliam who was secretary of the Cowdray hounds. The route zig-zags steeply downhill to old farm buildings in a spot which can be seriously muddy at the bottom of Westburton Hill; it then heads uphill on a narrow chalk track, passing a trig point at 178m and soon reaching the busy A29 Worthing road. Here the landscape dives down into the Arun valley, with dramatic chalk hills beyond Amberley signalling the next climb.

8. Cross the A29, and the bridleway that continues the route will be found a short distance to the south. For a pick-up by car, a convenient meeting place is the large car park at the roundabout where the A284 meets the A29 at Whiteways Lodge about two-thirds of a mile down the road. The SDW carries on steeply downhill by the side of Coombe Wood on another chalk track, bringing you to a lane a short way to the north of the hamlet of Houghton; here Charles II is reputed to have stopped at the George & Dragon pub while making his escape to France in the seventeenth century.

The much-improved SDW route now crosses the River Arun and the railway via two new bridleway bridges, emerging on the road uphill from Amberley, a hamlet which boasts a riverside cafe with outdoor seating, as well as a pub, restaurant, small shop, water trough with drinking tap and the famous Chalk Pits Museum.

9. The SDW continues steeply up High Titton Lane, before emerging on the open downs. A fenced track leads steeply uphill on grass away from Downs Farm towards Amberley Mount; after a stiff but ridable climb, the top of Rackham Hill is marked by a trig point at 193m, and with few trees on the hillsides the views are mostly unobstructed. To the west is Amberley Castle, once a fourteenth-century fortified manor house for the Bishops of Chichester, and now a luxury country house hotel. To the north lies Parham House, an Elizabethan mansion with wooded deer park. To the south is Arundel, an ancient town built on a hillside with its own fine castle and Roman Catholic cathedral of St Philip Neri. To the east, the downs and the route of the South Downs Way continue into the distance.

10. The SDW goes eastwards downhill to cross the dual carriageway A24. A safer alternative route diverts downhill to the north-east past Rowdell House, crossing the A24 by a footbridge, which brings you into Washington by the side of its church and not far from The Washington Inn.

From here a chalk track leads steeply up to the top of Chanctonbury Hill, passing a trig point at 238m on the way to Chanctonbury Ring, a mystic circle of trees which broods over the whole area. Originally a third to fourth-century Roman temple, the ring was planted with trees by Charles Goring in the late eighteenth century. Many of his trees were blown down by the great gale of 1987, but replanting has taken place. Just over two miles to the south the Iron Age hill fort of Cissbury Ring can sometimes also be seen.

11. The route turns south-east, following a wide chalk track on a slight downhill, giving very fast riding through open grassland. Steyning comes into view at the bottom of Steyning Round Hill, and is a good place to break the ride and maybe stay overnight. A concrete track leads steeply down the hillside from Steyning Bowl, where there is a small car park and an information board; this is about the halfway stage of this ride.

12. Past Steyning Bowl, the SDW turns left off the road, crossing a grassy field by the side of Annington Hill with the valley of the River Adur coming into sight ahead. This is the first great river crossing of the South Downs Way, and heralds the much more open country of the eastern part of the route. A hard track leads downhill, giving quite a fast descent, joining a narrow road by Annington Farm which heads east towards St Botolph's Church on the riverside. A hundred yards or so before the church, a track turns left to cross the river by a footbridge, close by a water

You will meet other riders, but few do the whole route.

tap and a noticeboard indicating the southern end of the Downs Link.

13. On the east side of the River Arun the route follows the A283 Shoreham road for a couple of hundred yards to the north, before turning right onto a track heading up the side of Beeding Hill. This leads to a narrow road on the top of the down, with a panoramic view of the valley behind; far beyond is the nineteenth-century chapel of Lancing College built high on a promontory. The road leads east along the top of this bleak down, passing Tottington Barn with its few protective conifers, the only Youth Hostel directly on the route of the South Downs Way.

From here the road becomes a track which gives good riding, passing the radio masts and the trig point at 216m on Truleigh Hill, and crossing National Trust land by an ancient motte and bailey by Edburton Hill. The route follows an up and down track towards Fulking Hill, above Fulking village where the Shepherd and Dog Inn has a freshwater spring gushing from the hillside.

14. Beyond Fulking Hill the route goes over open grassland towards the isolated Dyke Hotel (a public house) at the top of Devil's Dyke; this was given its name because in the mists of time the devil dug a dyke in the hillside in order to flood the surrounding country and its churches, but never finished the job!

The route joins the narrow road which connects the hotel to the outside world, with the dyke and its Iron Age enclosure below to the left. It leads on to a car park set in an area of shrub and woodland, where the SDW turns left downhill into the hamlet of Saddlescombe. Watch out here: although signposting for the SDW is generally excellent, this turning is not so obvious.

15. At the bottom of the hill a track leads off to the right past farm buildings, coming to a sunken track that heads up towards open downland above West Hill. Riding on along the top of the down, the route then heads downhill on a track, joining the A23 Brighton road at Pyecombe.

Here the SDW passes the church, turning right to cross the A273 Haywards Heath road, and then eastwards through the entrance gates of Pyecombe Golf Club a short way uphill. Past the club buildings you have to follow a fenced track along potentially muddy ground, and then the side of fields. Beyond New Barn Farm the twin Jack and Jill Clayton windmills come into view above Clayton village, one of the famous landmarks of the downs, but now no longer working.

16. The SDW carries on eastwards, passing the Keymer Post on the top of the down at 233m, close by dewponds and across grassland as it drops down to the trig point at the top of Ditchling Beacon (233m), one of the highest points of the South Downs Way and the site of an ancient hill fort where fires were lit to warn of the Spanish Armada – from here the North Downs can be seen on a clear day. A steep, narrow road connects Brighton with the village of Ditchling on

Typical South Downs Way scenery, as seen from the top of Steyning Bowl.

the north side of the downs, a place that has attracted many artists and craftsmen including the eccentric Eric Gill.

17. Past the Ditchling Beacon car park the SDW continues eastwards on a fast track over the grassy top of the downs, passing a V-shaped plantation designed to commemorate Queen Victoria's Jubilee; to the south, the enormous mass of Brighton dominates the coast. Just over two miles from Ditchling Beacon, the SDW takes a major change in direction, following the line of the downs to the south-east. However, first it turns to the south-west, leaving the track which goes straight ahead at a clearly signposted gate before Ashcombe Bottom, the only extensive patch of woodland on this part of the downs.

18. The route turns down a track with wire fences on either side, then bears left to head south-east down the side of a field, passing

beneath overhead cables. From here there are clear views over Lewes and its disused racecourse, looking out over an area where the Battle of Lewes was fought in 1264.

Along Balmer Down the route heads downhill towards woods, entering the Ashcombe plantation just before the A27 Lewes–Brighton road; on the far side is the Newmarket Inn and its neighbouring petrol station. The SDW passes close by these, through a railway arch and uphill on a chalk track, climbing the side of the valley by Loose Bottom. At the top it turns left by the Newmarket plantation, a grove of beeches, and left again by the side of Castle Hill; it then continues south-east towards Eastbourne, above the village of Kingston-near-Lewes.

19. The route crosses Swanborough Hill with views over Swanborough Manor below, once the grange of Lewes Priory and also owned by Sir Philip Sidney. On a windless day it is good riding

The riding can be hard and sometimes muddy, but the good view stays the same.

here, and the going is fast when you join the concrete track that runs straight as a dye along Itford Hill and Front Hill. From there, a narrow track leads along the side of woods at Mill Hill, coming to an unmade road which gives a fast ride down to the village of Rodmell. Here you will find Monk's House, once owned by Leonard and Virginia Woolf and now administered by the National Trust.

20. The South Downs Way crosses the River Ouse, where Virginia Woolf drowned herself in 1941 due to her fear of impending madness. The route follows the road south towards Newhaven, turning into Southease to follow the bridge over the Ouse, and skirting Southease railway station to reach the A26 Newhaven road by Itford Farm.

Turning right and running for a hundred yards or so down this road, the SDW then bears left up the side of Itford Hill on a chalk track; this curves its way up the hillside to head east past Red Lion and White Lion ponds, two dried-up

dew ponds. The downs here are dominated by the enormous radio mast on the top of Beddingham Hill at 190m; below is Beddingham itself, where a Roman villa was discovered as recently as 1987, part of the important network of old trading routes and posts which criss-crossed the region. A mile or so further north is Glyndebourne, the Elizabethan mansion which hosts the world famous Glyndebourne Opera season.

21. It's a good ride along the top of the downs here with big views on either side all the way. Riding on past the car park towards the trig point at Firle Beacon at 217m, the route passes a maze of tumuli with panoramic views for miles around. Turning to the right to head south-east, the SDW continues along the top of the downs, passing Charleston Farm to the north below, once the home of the artists Vanessa and Quentin Bell. More tumuli give an interesting variation to the landscape, then the route heads downhill on a fast fenced track via Long Burgh towards the village of Alfriston on the banks of the River Cuckmere. The SDW emerges in the main street by the Star Inn; the large church here is known as 'the Cathedral of the South Downs', and has a handsome green which is a good place to picnic.

22. From Alfriston the final section of the South Downs Way splits: riders must continue inland over the downs on a fairly direct bridleway route, while walkers can follow the coastal path along the cliff tops of the Seven Sisters Country Park which is footpath all the way. The bridleway route leads steeply up the hill behind Alfriston, following a hard chalk track. If you take a look at the northern side of this hill you will see the Long Man of Wilmington, a gigantic human figure cut into the turf, some 226ft (68.5m) long and first recorded in the mid-eighteenth century.

At the top of the hill there is a view over the huge bowl of Tenantry Ground, and from here the route crosses open grassland, with direction markers showing the way as it curves round to the south. It enters woodland, descending on a narrow, rutted track to the hamlet of Jevington where the Hawthorn Lodge tea rooms are handily situated at the foot of the last climb of the SDW.

23. It's not a bad climb from Jevington, and once on top the route follows a hard track across level ground, passing the Eastbourne Downs golf course to the right with Eastbourne itself laid out at the foot of the down to the left.

On reaching the A259 this track continues straight ahead, before sweeping eastwards downhill into Eastbourne on a great descent, finishing on the outskirts of the town at Paradise Way.

Slow down for other users of the South Downs Way.

Places To Visit:
Queen Elizabeth Country Park
(tel: 01705 595040);
Uppark NT (tel: 01730 825317);
Bignor Roman Villa (tel: 017987 259);
Weald & Downland Open Air Museum
(tel: 01243 811348);
Parham House & Gardens
(tel: 01903 744888);
Arundel Castle (tel: 01903 883136);
Amberley Chalk Pits Museum
(tel: 01798 831370);
The Monk's House NT
(tel: 01892 890651);
Alfriston Clergy House NT
(tel: 01323 870001).

Top Pubs:
The Ship at South Harting;
The Bridge Inn at Amberley;
The Castle Hotel at Bramber;
The Star Inn at Alfriston.

From Queen Elizabeth Country Park

Mainly Offroad

Area: The west end of the South Downs, to the south of Petersfield.

OS Map: Landranger 197 Chichester and The Downs.

Route:
Queen Elizabeth Country Park (GR:718185)
Chalton (GR:732161)
West Marden (GR:773135)
Walderton (793107)
South Downs Way (GR:772191)
Queen Elizabeth Country Park (GR:718185)

Nearest BR Stations:
Petersfield/ Rowlands Castle.

Approx Length: 26 miles (42km).

Time: Allow 4 hours.

Rating: Moderate in dry weather; terrible if there's a lot of mud. No severe hills on main circuit, but the purpose designed mountain bike track at Queen Elizabeth Country Park (QEP) is very challenging if ridden hard.

Heading for the hills beyond Chalton.

Queen Elizabeth Country Park is a good place to start this ride, but if you arrive by car you have to pay for the car park; it can get crowded in summer, so get there early.

QEP is managed by the Forestry Commission and features a huge maze of very hilly tracks and trails. These are used by walkers, horse-riders and mountain bikers, but due to conflict of use mountain bikers are asked to stick to the special three-mile (4.8km) signposted mountain bike track which despite its short length is very challenging with some severe ups and downs; when starting this circuit, it may be best left until the end of the day.

1. To leave QEP, follow the main track north-eastwards to the top of the hill between War Down and Holt Down, and then follow the hillside down the other side (bridleway) to the

From Queen Elizabeth Country Park

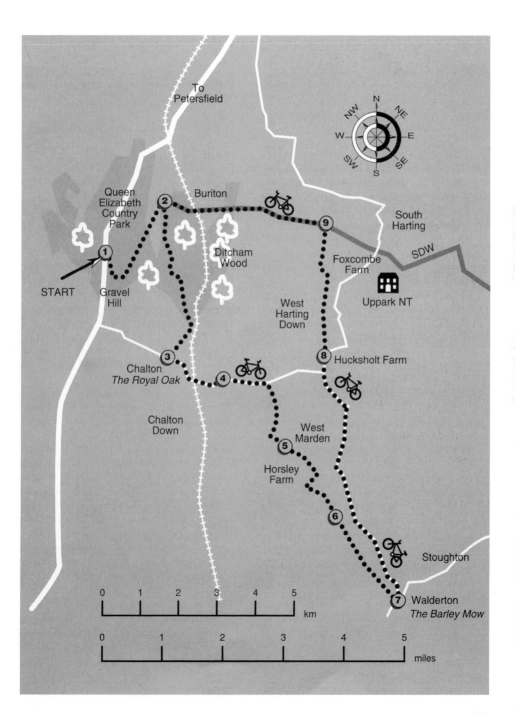

Forestry Commission car park at the foot of War Down (GR:734197), half a mile south-west of Buriton. Despite the fact that this is a main through route to the South Downs way, it is not clearly signposted and some care is neeed with the OS map to ensure you are on course.

2. Turn right out of the car park, and follow the road south towards Chalton. It's an enjoyable ride past peaceful woods and fields, mainly downhill, and little used by cars out of the summer season. Ride under the overhead powerlines, following the road as it comes alongside the railway. As it swings away, look out for a couple of houses on the left. Opposite, on the right, an unmarked track leads up the hillside. This is a byway which offers a short cut offroad to Chalton; follow it to the top of the hill, then turn right along the road and steeply downhill into Chalton, where The Royal Oak awaits in a pleasant setting across the green from the village church.

3. Head back up the hill, going eastwards out of Chalton. At the top of the hill follow a steep downhill, to the south, bearing east to cross the railway line. Go straight ahead to join an unmarked track which heads due east. After a slight uphill the going is good as it heads between woods and fields towards Cowdown Farm.

4. After passing a disused building on the right, look out for a bridleway crossroads, a mile and a half or so from the road; the signpost on the right is well hidden, so take it easy here. Turn right downhill across a big open field, crossing another field on a slight uphill where depending on conditions the riding may range from easy to difficult.

The bridleway goes straight ahead into a belt of trees, and up to the road. Cross straight over here, following the bridleway uphill across a field (liable to be heavy going), and then bearing right up the hillside into trees on a fairly steep uphill. At the top follow the track through the woods, taking the right turn just past the overhead powerlines, and then turning left out of the woods at a bridleway T-junction.

5. Follow this old green lane south-eastwards between hedges – parts of the route can be muddy. Take the right turn past Horsley Farm (disused, but ready for conversion), and follow the hard track straight ahead towards the road.

If you wish to cut the ride short at this point, just past Horsley Farm follow a bridleway track-downhill to the left, and then follow the road down into West Marden.

6. Turn left at the road, and then take the next right turn. This starts to go downhill along Nore Down. When you come to a belt of trees on the right, bear right onto the bridleway as signposted, which leads along the top of the hillside called Watergate Hanger. It can be extremely muddy here in wet weather when it is recommended that you cut out this part of the route or follow the road to Walderton.

Halfway along Watergate Hanger, the track comes out of the trees by a solitary house to the north-east of Broadreed Farm. Join the hard track which follows the side of the woods, continuing in the same south-easterly direction.

7. The track leads down to a lane, and then steeply downhill to join the B2146 road in the valley bottom. Bear right and then left for a visit to the pub at Walderton.

From here, retrace your wheel tracks to the B2146, and then follow it northwards, passing through West Marden and Compton. After approximately four miles on-road and a mile or so past Compton, look for a bridleway track leading past Hucksholt Farm on the left, as the road bears right on a steady uphill.

8. This track leads due north for just over two miles to join the South Downs Way, passing through open fields and then going through the side of extensive woodland on West Harting Down. Most of the way it's fairly flat and fast riding. At Foxcombe Farm go straight ahead on a slight uphill, passing a few houses and turning

The start of the purpose-designed mountain bike trail at Queen Elizabeth Country Park. It's a tough course!

left onto the South Downs Way at a bridleway crossroads.

9. From here it's approximately three miles to QEP. This section of the SDW goes on-road at Sunwood Farm, and then back offroad at Coulters Farm, crossing the railway and leading downhill on-road to the Forestry Commision car park at the bottom of War Down. Go through the gate and bear left up the hill here, to find your way back into QEP; or if you're desperate for a pub, turn right down the hill into Buriton.

Places To Visit:
Queen Elizabeth Country Park
(tel: 01705 595040).

Top Pubs:
The Royal Oak at Chalton;
The Barley Mow at Walderton;
The Victoria at West Marden;
seasonal cafe at QEP.

Kingley Vale and Stansted

The Stoughton Down car park at the foot of Lambdown Hill, halfway between Stoughton and East Marden, is a good place to start this ride if you arrive by car; alternatively try the Kingley Vale car park at West Stoke, which is considerably smaller and popular with weekend walkers.

1. From the Stoughton Down CP go through the gate, and onto a hard gravel forest track leading north-east by the side of woods at the bottom of Lambdown Hill. Follow this track as it bears round to the right and starts to head uphill through the woods; the official bridleway then goes straight up the hillside, while the forestry road winds its way up and is less steep but longer, joining it further up the hillside by a bridleway crossroads at Long Barrows.

2. Follow the bridleway straight ahead to the south here, ignoring turnings to left (uphill) and right (downhill). After a slight descent, the track climbs easily up to the top of Kingley Vale where you break out onto an open plateau notable for three tumuli at Cross Dyke.

On a clear day this is a wonderful spot to stop and take in the landscape, with great views over Chichester harbour and beyond to the Isle of Wight. Riding over the tumuli used to be fun but no longer seems a good idea, as these ancient monuments are suffering notable erosion. Don't do it!

3. From the westernmost tumuli, two tracks lead westwards along the top of the down. It doesn't matter which you take; their condition varies depending on how muddy it is, and how much they've been trampled by horses. Both tracks break out of the woods with an open field ahead. Turn left onto the track here, and follow it down the side of the field, bearing right and going round the side of the field, with Kingley Vale's famous ancient forest of yew trees downhill to the left.

4. From here, the track heads westwards again, leading through trees and then breaking

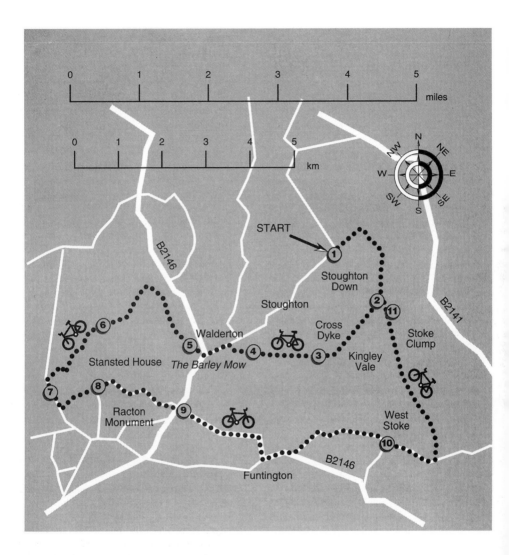

out into the open at the top of Walderton Down where there's a wonderful downhill to an isolated, disused barn. A quick right turn and then a left takes you to another long downhill through trees towards Walderton. Slam on the brakes at the bottom, and bear right past a gate on a much rougher track to join the road on the outskirts of Walderton.

5. Turn left past the pub in its pleasant village setting, and ride on to join the B2146. Turn right here, and then immediately left by a small group of houses; this leads to a fairly steep uphill. Near the top, look for a bridleway forking off to the right and take the left-hand track; this leads to the top of Watergate Hanger, with the wooded hillside dropping away to the right and an open field to the left.

6. Follow this hard track to an isolated house halfway along the top of the Hanger. Turn left and follow the track past Broadreed Farm, going straight on to join a tarmac road (bridleway) past the imposing house at Lumley Seat. Keep straight on until Stansted House (stately home with pleasant gardens; open during the summer) comes into view on the left.

7. If conditions are wet, follow the drive out to the road on the south-east corner of Stansted Forest. If they are reasonably dry, you can follow the bridleway which is signposted past the front of Stansted House; this gives a fine view of this imposing building, but it can be impossibly muddy in wet weather.

8. From here, follow the bridleway signpost out to the road. Turn left along the road, passing the Stansted gatehouse, then turn left off the road at the next bridleway signpost to join the Sussex Border Path heading east towards Racton Monument. The going can be muddy along here in wet weather, but in dry conditions it's very pleasant riding. The monument is an enormous empty tower, a 'folly' which its present owner hopes to turn into a house. One hopes it will always remains a folly, as its original builder intended.

9. Ride past the monument and on down the hill, to join the road at the junction of the B2146 and B2147. Cross straight over onto the B2146, with a moderate uphill and then a steady downhill taking you as far as Funtington, where there is a roadside pub.

From here, follow the B2146 through the village (a short section of quite busy road), forking left onto an unmarked lane at the end of the houses. Follow this lane past Wood End and the West Stoke car park at the foot of Kingley Vale (an alternative start point). Ride on through West Stoke, and look out for the tiny village hall which serves teas on summer weekends - a nice place to stop.

10. Past the last houses that make up West Stoke, turn left offroad at the next bridleway sign. Go through the gate and follow the steep and steady track uphill to the ancient circle of trees at Stoke Clump. The views from here are very fine, and if you're riding in the other direction it makes a great downhill. However it's also popular with dog walkers; please slow right down if you see any.

Past Stoke Clump the track narrows and can be badly stirred up by horses, and is occasionally impossibly muddy. It leads downhill to a bridleway crossroads on the south-east side of Kingley Vale. Ride straight on up the hill ahead, and pace yourself, as it's extremely difficult to make it to the top without putting a foot down. At first it's steady but strength sapping; then when it enters the Kingley Vale area it gets much steeper with the track badly eroded.

11. When you reach the bridleway crossroads at the top, turn right and follow the track to the north along Bow Hill, with fine views over to St Roche's Hill at Goodwood with the South Downs beyond. Follow the track straight on past Goosehill Camp and the isolated house in the trees – once a smallpox hospital and now a retreat – to join a hard track which leads through the woods to a gate, and on to a bridleway crossroads.

A right turn leads steeply downhill to the super smart pub at Chilgrove; a left turn takes you on a fast downhill past magnificent beech trees, and then to the Stoughton Down car park start point.

Places To Visit:
Stansted House (tel: 01705 412265).

Top Pubs:
The Barley Mow at Walderton;
The White Horse at Chilgrove;
The Fox and Hounds at Funtington.

The view from the top of Kingley Vale.

A variety of tracks lead up to the top of Kingley Vale.

The Kingley Vale tumuli are an important landmark.

Stop for a rest at the Barley Mow.

Goodwood and the Downs

Mainly Offroad

Area: The western end of the South Downs, near Goodwood.

OS Map: Landranger 197 Chichester and The Downs.

Route:
Goodwood Country Park CP (GR:890110)
The Trundle/St Roche's Hill (GR:878110)
West Dean (GR:857123)
Chilgrove (GR:828145)
Hooksway (GR:815162)
Linch Down/SDW (GR:845173)
Cocking/SDW (GR:875166)
Charlton Forest/SDW (GR:900165)
Charlton (GR:889129)
Goodwood Country Park CP (GR:890110)

Nearest BR Stations: Chichester.

Approx Length: 24 miles (39km).

Time: Allow 4–6 hours.

Rating: Moderate/Hard. Four good climbs up St Roche's Hill, Linch Down (SDW), Manorfarm Down (SDW), Charlton Park.

There are extensive car parks along the south side of Goodwood racecourse which makes this a good place to start from. They are usually empty, though keep well away on race days when you will find the whole area packed – you may even decide to forget the ride and try your luck on the horses!

1. Follow the road westwards, turning right at a T-junction with the Goodwood grandstand on your right. Near the top of the hill bear left onto a bridleway, joining a narrow track which scrambles up the side of St Roche's Hill. Near the top the bridleway goes through a gate and out onto the side of the hill, with the Trundle radio masts on the hilltop to the right; if you are interested in prehistory, it's worth leaving your bike and walking to the top where there are the clearly defined ramparts and ditches of a huge circular hill fort.

2. Follow the track on down the side of St Roche's Hill, keeping westwards and dropping down to the gate where there is a small car park at the top of the road that leads up from Singleton. Ride straight ahead here, passing an empty house on the right (which had been sold by auction at the time of writing), and bearing right on a bridleway which drops down the side of the hill heading north-west towards West Dean. It runs past the walls of the West Dean estate, and then drops down to West Dean itself, a neat riverside hamlet which is well worth a quick tour.

3. Ride straight on, past the West Dean post office/general stores, and cross the main A286 by the pub. The narrow road passes under a railway arch, then twists and turns through delightful countryside, at last levelling out on a long straight to Colworth Down.

Follow this very quiet road – one suspects few cars know it exists – beneath the overhead powerlines, following Westdean Woods on the right to Stapleash Farm. Turn right with the road here, and ride on down through Chilgrove, joining the B2141 road by The White Hart pub.

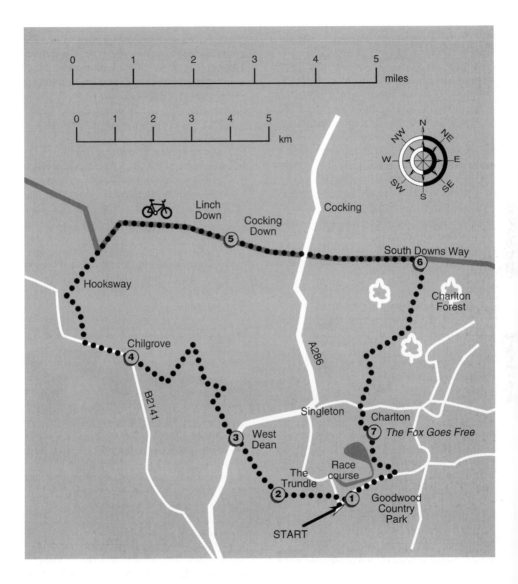

4. Turn right along the B2141 which heads westwards on a steady uphill. After a few hundred yards, look out for a bridleway track forking off to the right. This leads down the side of the hill – expect huge puddles in wet weather at the bottom – and then along the side of Phillis Wood to The Royal Oak at Hooksway.

From The Royal Oak, head north-eastwards up the hillside, taking the right-hand track of two signposted bridleways. It's a steady climb up through woodland to join the South Downs Way, passing the back of Monkton House and then riding eastwards along the top of Linch Down at a high point of the SDW.

5. The SDW drops steeply down the side of Cocking Down, passing a conveniently signposted pub at Cocking before reaching the A286 by a small car park (GR:876166). Cross straight over the road and continue along the SDW on a track which heads steeply uphill past Hill Barn Farm (note the convenient public water tap here) to the top of Heyshott Down; the trig point to the left of the track is at a height of 233m.

6. Past the trig point, turn off at the next bridleway signposted to the right. This leads downhill through Charlton Forest, and through open fields at North Down. Keep straight on along this track which swings south into Charlton: the pub here is The Fox Goes Free.

7. From the pub, cross the road and follow the lane ahead round to the right, bearing left past Fox Hall to join a bridleway track heading up the hillside past Charlton Park. At the top this emerges by the eastern end of the Goodwood racecourse, and there are various unmarked tracks on the south side of the road which allow you to finish this ride offroad.

Places To Visit:
Goodwood Racecourse
(tel: 01243 774107);
Goodwood House (tel: 01243 774107);
Weald and Downland Museum,
Singleton (tel: 01243 811348).

Top Pubs:
The White Horse at Chilgrove;
The Royal Oak at Hooksway;
The Fox Goes Free at Charlton;
also pub stops at West Dean and Cocking.

Just before you cross the A286, a bridleway diversion leads to the Blue Bell Inn at Cocking.

Selhurst Park and The Downs

Mainly Offroad

Area: The western end of the South Downs, to the north-east of Goodwood.

OS Map: Landranger 197 Chichester and The Downs.

Route:
Selhurst Park CP (GR:926118)
Burton Down/SDW (GR:965131)
Littleton Farm/SDW (GR:951143)
Graffham Down/SDW (GR:926161)
East Dean (GR:904130)
Selhurst Park CP (GR:926118)

Nearest BR Stations: Amberley/ Chichester.

Approx Length: 12 miles (19km).

Time: Allow 3 hours.

Rating: Moderate. One big climb up Littleton Down (SDW).

Eartham Woods are best tackled in dry weather.

There is a large, free car parking area at Selhurst Park, on the north side of the road that leads eastwards from Goodwood to join the A285. Alternatively you could start this ride from the Bignor Hill car park, which is at the eastern end of the ride on top of the SDW (GR:973129).

1. From the Selhurst Park car park turn left along the road, which is usually quiet and pleasant riding. Head east, crossing straight over the A285 with care, to join a bridleway track that continues eastwards past a couple of houses on the corner.

Follow this track uphill through Eartham Woods; this is a fine area for riding with a mass of trails that can, however, become confusing. Follow the main trail out of the woods and onto Burton Down, joining the South Downs Way below the twin radio masts on the summit.

Ride on as far as the car park on top of the

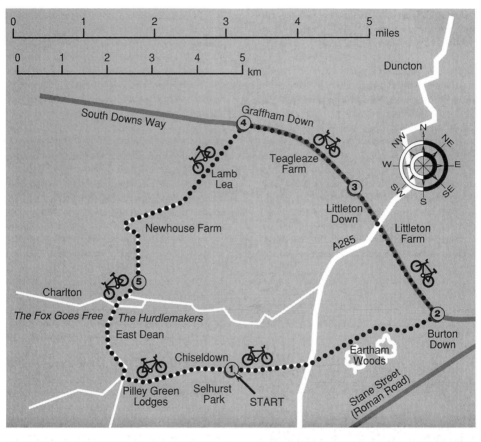

The Fox Goes Free at Charlton makes a good place to stop.

downs at Bignor Hill - this would make a good optional start point for the ride; it attracts plenty of weekend car-borne strollers, so take care.

2. At the Bignor Hill car park turn north-west to pass close by the twin radio masts, taking the next left turn south-west to rejoin the SDW. There are fine views all round from here. Follow the SDW to the north-west on what can be a very fast downhill, until you reach the A285 in the valley.

Cross straight over the A285, and follow the SDW track up the other side; it bears right past some houses and crosses an open field where it goes steeply uphill with fine views opening out behind. The bridleway then continues to climb up Littleton Down, joining a good track on the top of Woolavington Down.

The twin radio masts at the top of Bignor Hill.

3. Ride on past the ancient Tegleaze signpost, passing Tegleaze Farm which is down the hillside on the left – it is the only dwelling so high on this part of the downs. When fields start to open out on the left side of the track, look out for the next bridleway crossroads; this is clearly signposted to East Dean and Graffham, at the top of Graffham Down.

4. Turn left downhill off the SDW here, following the track through the woods and crossing straight over the main forestry road.

Continue downhill through Lamb Lea, breaking out of the trees and joining a farm lane in the valley by a disused barn. Follow this lane along the valley to Newhouse Farm, joining the road to head due south to the village of East Dean where a good pub awaits.

5. From East Dean follow the road uphill, signposted for Chichester. At the top, turn left for the Selhurst Park car park.

Alternatively, turn left out of East Dean, following the road westwards signposted to Charlton. This leads to The Fox Goes Free; from here, cross straight over the road, following the lane ahead to join a bridleway track which goes southwards up the hillside, passing under powerlines and emerging at the top between Charlton Park and Goodwood racecourse. Bear left onto the road here, riding east to the Selhurst Park car park just over two miles distant.

Places To Visit:
Goodwood Country Park
(tel: 01243 774107).

Top Pubs:
The Fox Goes Free at Charlton;
The Hurdlemakers at East Dean.

Bignor Hill and the Downs

Mainly Offroad

Area: From the South Downs north towards Fittleworth and Petworth.

OS Map: Landranger 197 Chichester and The Downs

Route:
Bignor Hill (GR:973129)
Duncton (GR:961175)
Heath End (GR:967188)
Fittleworth (GR:010190)
Sutton (GR:982152)
Bignor Hill (GR:973129)

Nearest BR Station: Amberley.

Approx Length: 14 miles (23km).

Time: Allow 3 hours.

Rating: Moderate. Some good climbs; parts of the route can be muddy.

This is a good tour of the downland south of Petworth, climbing up and down to join the South Downs Way. The ride could just as easily be started from any of the villages around the circuit, and with such a good selection of pubs could even be slowed to a pedalled pub crawl!

It also connects neatly with the railway at Amberley, which is just over four miles off-circuit via a very pleasant section of the South Downs Way.

1. Starting from the Bignor Hill car park leaves the big climbs until last; it's your choice! If you prefer to start on low ground, Duncton or Fittleworth would work equally well.

From the Bignor Hill car park, take the hard track that heads north-west on the east side of the two radio masts; this is not the South Downs Way, and is consequently less used by walking/riding 'traffic'. Once past the masts it's downhill all the way, with a fast descent on hard chalk leading past woodland with some good views over the rest of the route to the north.

2. Everything is well signposted here, but you still need to keep an eye on the map and the signposts as the track heads north by the side of Farm Hill and Barlavington Down. There are some ups as well as downs, but it's all really delightful riding – fork right onto the track which swings north-east and down through the woods, emerging into the open to cross a couple of fields before hitting a lane just west of Barlavington.

3. Cross straight over here, joining a bridle-way track that bears left towards trees, and then right on a steady downhill to cross the ponds by St Michael's Burton Park, a huge classical pile which was a school. Ride past the front of the main building and its chapel, bearing right and left to continue due north on a good, hard track which leads to a lane by Heath End; cross straight over here, and the bridleway connects with the main A285 Petworth road.

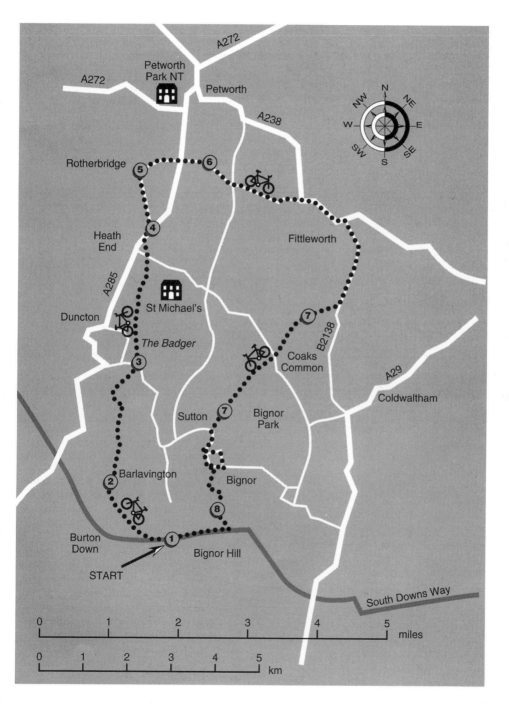

St. Michael's Burton Park - the route leads close to the main buildings.

4. The A285 is not too congested, and it's only a short distance downhill northwards to the next bridleway turn-off, just past the old railway along a lane to the left. Alternatively, if you ride on down to the river you will come to The Badger, one of the best pubs in the whole area; just beyond there are some interesting old waterworks at Coultershaw Bridge, occasionally open to the public on summer Sundays.

5. Back to the bridleway, the lane turns to a track which runs past Kilsham Farm to Rotherbridge; this appears to be little more than one lovely house by the side of the River Rother in a very pleasant setting. Turn right with the track towards the road (ignore the bridleway

sign pointing north ahead) and cross back over the A285 about one mile south of Petworth; alternatively you might like to investigate this interesting small town with its famous National Trust house and huge deer park.

6. Follow the road for just over three miles into Fittleworth, bearing south on the B2138 to re-cross the River Rother; despite being on-road, this is all quite pleasant riding.

Go past the disused railway line ignoring the first right turning, and look for the next lane on the right to Tripphill Farm. Ride on past the farm, and join a potentially muddy track (after wet weather) which leads south-west across Coates Common.

Approaching Bignor Park, with the Downs still ahead.

8. Stop awhile to gaze at Bignor Park – it could be your kind of house – then you can either join a lane at Sutton where you can divert to the pub, or bear left and head on south towards Bignor where there is a short, sharp, on-road climb. Bignor is famous for its Roman villa (on the east side) which is open to the public; to the south a dead-end road snakes up the side of the down towards the Bignor Hill car park: this is where you are heading.

9. Occasional cars can be an annoyance on this steep, windy, narrow road, and it's a relief to fork off onto the bridleway track that bears left through the woods; the route steadily gains height on a good surface on the hillside, then drops down to join the South Downs Way at the foot of Westburton Hill. But what goes down must go up, and you've had your down-hills. From here on it's up, up, up!

Follow the SDW as it zig-zags up the side of Bignor Hill, with the twin radio masts guiding you back to the top.

> *Places To Visit:*
> Petworth House and Park NT
> (tel: 01798 42207);
> Bignor Roman Villa
> (tel: 017987 259).
>
> *Top Pubs:*
> The Badger at Duncton;
> The White Horse at Sutton.

7. This is a pleasant area for walking and horses; but not so good for mountain bikes as there is too much sandy soil for good traction; the going improves further on however.

The track leads to a lane where you cross over onto another bridleway which continues south-west all the way to Sutton with views of the downs looming ahead. Some of the going along here is alright, and if you were on a horse it would rate as a very pleasant track, but for bikers parts are severely churned up by hooves – even in dry weather – and it is virtually impossible to ride the whole distance.

River Arun Ride

Mainly Offroad

Area: The South Downs, to the north of Arundel.

OS Map: Landranger 197 Chichester and the Downs.

Route:
Arundel (GR:020070)
Slindon (GR:970085)
Stane Street (GR:951113)
The South Downs Way/Bignor Hill (GR:982131)
Houghton (GR:016118)
Arundel (GR:020070)

Nearest BR Stations:
Arundel/Amberley.

Approx Length: 15 miles (24km).

Time: Allow 3 hours, plus time to stop and look around.

Rating: Moderate. Be prepared for some mud if it's wet, some ups and downs, and a tricky ride by the River Arun.

This is an excellent ride, starting and finishing in the historic city of Arundel and taking in a section of the South Downs Way, with offroad riding for 90 per cent of the route, culminating in an interesting, though somewhat technical ride along the banks of the River Arun. Be warned that parts of the ride have the potential to be seriously muddy, so think twice about starting after a spell of wet weather.

1. Arundel is a very interesting small city with lots to look at, including a cathedral and its own splendid castle which dominates the town from the hillside. From the Information Centre, find your way to the main roundabout at the intersection of the A27 and A284. About fifty yards along the A27 going west (Chichester direction), cross over to the north side of the road, and go up the unmarked driveway ahead between the lodges on the corner.

2. A short way on, take the bridleway track signposted off to the left. This leads straight into Screens Wood, following a wide track through the trees; this is likely to be seriously muddy if there has been any rain – you have been warned! Further on, the track breaks out of the trees and becomes more bike friendly, turning left out of the woods by a padlocked gate and crossing a field to join another track across open country on the way to Rewell House. This section is all fast riding on level ground, leading past the back of Rewell House into Rewell Wood on a hard track. Keep straight on over the first crossing track, and then go past the second forestry crossing track with its sign saying 'No Horses'.

3. Some way on you come to bridleway signs pointing right and straight ahead, just below Rewell Hill. Go straight ahead, following the track round to the left and onto an increasingly fast downhill. The track breaks out of the woods on a fast, bumpy surface, then re-enters the woods, coming to a dark hollow. Signposting is somewhat lacking here and the way is not too

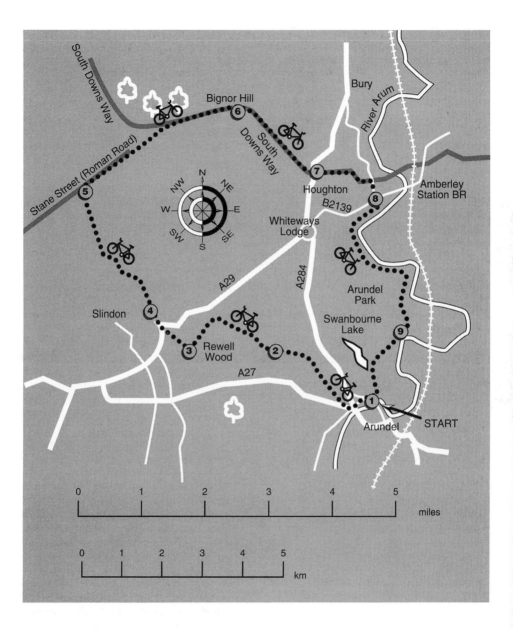

obvious; turn sharp right for more downhill riding, following the woodland track on past a summer camp site, and you should come out onto the A29 just east of Slindon.

4. Go straight over here but take care: it's a dangerous road to cross, with a blind bend and cars going seriously fast in both directions. Go up the short lane ahead, and look for the bridle-

Arundel Castle is well worth a visit and dominates the town built round it.

way that goes straight ahead into the woods. (If you want to visit the village of Slindon which has a pleasant pub, turn left along the road here; a bridleway reconnects with the route.) Follow the narrow track through the trees; this is another section that can be muddy. It leads out to open country over Little Down, and here you must be careful to keep heading north, before following the track left (westwards) to join a narrow tarmac lane close by the trig point at the folly on the opposite hillside. Ride northwards along this lane for a hundred yards or so, then fork left onto the bridleway that follows the track ahead past a gate. This is good riding, leading along a dead-straight trail with tall trees on either side, heading into North Wood with Eartham Wood beyond.

5. After riding on this track for a mile or so you come to an ancient five-way signpost which

indicates the route of the Roman road known as Stane Street, which once ran all the way between Chichester and the Roman villa at Bignor, connecting them to settlements beyond. To follow Stane Street, take the track signposted for Bignor. Although a bridleway it is fairly narrow so let walkers or horse-riders come by; and riding is also made difficult by old gnarled roots lying across the surface. After a time this track breaks out into the open across a field, passing Gumber Farm (where there is 'bothy' overnight accommodation) in a hollow then heading steadily uphill; the radio masts at the top of Burton Down mark the highest point of the downs in this area.

6. Keep straight on ahead, ignoring crossing tracks, and what remains of Stane Street will eventually bring you up to the car park on top of Bignor Hill. Turn right here for a fast pedal eastwards along the South Downs Way. As with any ride along this well-used LDP, remember that the sections near car parks can get congested, so take it very easy where there are walkers about. A good track leads steadily uphill with fine views on both sides of the downs, then swings sharply and steeply down to the farmstead at the bottom of Westburton Hill (it can be horribly muddy down here); and steadily uphill again until the track levels out and brings you to the A29.

7. This is an extremely busy road. The easiest way to get across is to turn right down the verge, and after seventy-five metres or so cross straight over to the South Downs Way sign on the other side. This leads you on a hard chalk track heading steeply down by the side of Coombe Wood, with great views ahead over the Arun valley to the continuation of the downs beyond Amberley where the chalk cliffs rise out of the plain. This is a steep, fast descent which takes you towards the village of Houghton which is along the road to the right; or you could turn left to cross the bridge into Amberley where you'll find a cafe and restaurant, as well as the famous Chalk Pits Industrial Museum.

8. To continue, cross straight over the B2139 to a dead-end lane; the big house up the road to the right is owned by Anita Roddick of Body Shop fame. This lane leads downhill past some cottagey houses to a narrow track that follows the side of the River Arun; a short way along there is a clearing under the cliffs on the right-hand side which makes a good place to stop for a picnic. Although this part of the route looks short and easy on the map, in practice it is pretty slow going. The riverside track is narrow and tortuous – few horses would risk coming along here – and on summer weekends it is likely to be popular with walkers, so take it easy. Some way further on, the bridleway heads up the hillside away from the river, following the side of fields, and this is much easier riding. The track leads on to the tiny select hamlet of South Stoke – stop and have a look at the wonderful archi-

Most of the route is well signposted.

tecture of the buttressed old barn here – and then across the open plain to Offham.

9. At Offham the track joins the road, passing the Black Rabbit Inn which enjoys an extremely pleasant riverside position. Further along the road the Wildfowl Reserve is a popular place with visitors; then after a mile or so you are back beneath the battlements of the castle and heading into Arundel, a town which is as nice a place as any to finish off a ride.

Places To Visit:
Arundel Castle (tel: 01903 883136);
Arundel Cathedral (tel: 01903 882297);
Amberley Chalk Pits Museum
(tel: 01798 831370).

Top Pubs:
The Black Rabbit at Offham;
The Spur at Slindon;
The Black Horse at Amberley;
The George and Dragon at Houghton.

Chanctonbury and Cissbury Rings

Mainly Offroad

Area: The South Downs to the north of Worthing.

OS Maps: Landrangers 197/198 Chichester/Brighton and the Downs.

Route:
Arundel (GR:020070)
Warningcamp (GR:035075)
High Salvington (GR:124067)
Cissbury Ring (GR:140080)
Chanctonbury Ring (GR:140120)
Springhead Hill GR:065125)
Burpham (GR:040089)
Arundel (GR:020070)

Nearest BR Station: Arundel.

Approx Length: 31 miles (50km).

Time: Allow 5 hours.

Rating: Moderate. Be prepared for some good climbs and potential mud.

This is a great ride on one of the most interesting parts of the South Downs, visiting two very ancient hill forts and taking in a good slice of the South Downs Way. If possible keep a ride like this to a weekday when fewer people are about; the tracks and trails here are popular, and you should be prepared to take your time as required.

1. Arundel is a fine place to start this ride from with its castle and cathedral dominating the town, and there is good parking plus the benefit of a railway station. However, if it is the wrong side of the route for you there are alternative start points along the circuit.

Follow the road out of Arundel onto the A27 going east towards Brighton; it's a short distance before you can turn left onto a lane, just past the railway. Follow this quiet lane through Warningcamp (where there is a YHA hostel, tel: 01903 882204), and then look out for a bridleway track on the right that goes into the woods at Warningcamp Hill. The first part can be pretty churned up by horses, but further on it is lovely riding, following the tracks and trails east into Wepham Wood.

2. You will need to keep an eye on the OS map here, taking a signposted right fork uphill (very difficult to ride up) into the woodland and then joining a series of wide forestry tracks which are great in dry weather but can be appallingly muddy if it's wet. Cross over the tarmac lane at Angmering Park, and keep straight on eastwards. Where the track bends round to the right, keep an eye out for the signposted bridleway crossroads; take a left here, heading downhill on a narrow track and across a field to join the lane at Michelgrove.

3. Turn left here, riding up past a very smart bungalow; then turn right through its old kitchen garden, following the bridleway sign along the side of the high walls and across fields onto Landranger 198.

Keep straight ahead, and you will come to

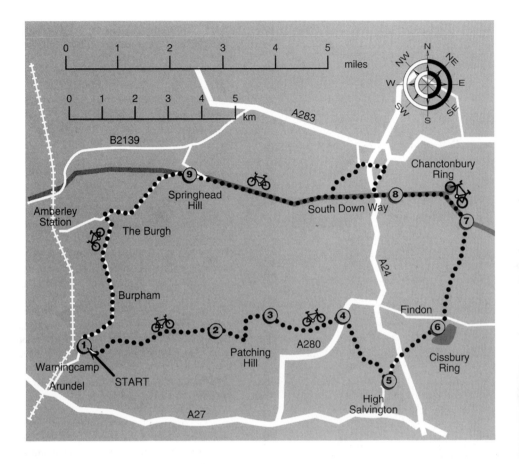

Myrtle Grove Farm situated in productive surroundings; here you bear right with the tarmac driveway, leaving it when you come to a crossing drive to go straight ahead across fields.

The bridleway here isn't too obvious – when I last rode by the whole of one field had been oversown – but just plug on to the top of the hill; from here you will see the track that heads down and then up by the side of Tolmare Farm ahead.

4. Cut across the A280 here, going straight onto the bridleway track on the other side. This soon leads up and away from the road, following tracks south-east past a radio mast to the

windmill at High Salvington. There is a car park on top here, making it a good alternative place to start the ride (GR:121072); however being close to the outskirts of Worthing, it is also a popular place with dog-walkers, which means you may need to slow right down.

5. At the windmill, turn left onto the road and follow it steeply downhill past another car park. It's a fast descent all the way, although when you hit the bottom, crossing the busy A24 can take time! The next section of bridleway goes straight ahead up to Cissbury Ring. Time needs to be taken here as well; the first part is only one person's width and it is very popular

Chanctonbury Ring, an ancient hill fort decorated with trees, high on the Downs.

with walkers (there is another car park here), leaving no room for unruly bikes. If there are a lot of people, just get off and walk.

6. When the narrow track breaks out of the trees the route becomes more open, but Cissbury Ring is always popular because there is yet another car park by its side (GR:139085) which could also be an alternative start point). You can ride up to the Ring itself, but *never* ride on the old ramparts, and *do* leave your bike outside. The Ring is a magical place on a fine day with huge views all around, but is at its best when there is no one else to bother you.

7. Looking north, you will see the trees which circle Chanctonbury Ring, the next stop on this ride. This is another magical place on the South Downs, planted by an eighteenth-century romantic who decided he would like to decorate the ancient hill fort with trees. Follow the hard chalk track northwards and then bear left onto the South Downs Way; most of it is steady uphill, but like any ride you have to take the

Arundel's Roman Catholic cathedral is one of many fine buildings in this old town.

rough with the smooth.

8. Past Chanctonbury Ring, the South Downs Way continues west, passing the trig point (238m) at Cross Dyke on a fast downhill where you must be careful to keep straight on, rather than swinging onto the left-side track.

From there, it is steep downhill all the way – too steep for speed near the bottom – to the A24. Divert down the lane to the right if you want to visit the pub in Washington, and find your way back onto the SDW by the narrow walker/rider A24 bridge; or cross straight over, and bear right up the other side, going steeply up Barnsfarm and Sullington Hill and back onto Landranger 197.

9. From here the ride along the SDW is pleasant enough, with steady ups and downs. Having done this section many times before and seeking out quieter tracks and trails, I opted to turn off onto the track which races southwards down to Lee Farm. This route starts brilliantly, but gets confusing south of Wepham Down.

Try it if you like, but my recommendation would be to keep on along the SDW, passing the car park at the top of Springhead Hill (GR:0711240) and taking the next bridleway track on the left about half a mile on. This heads down past The Burgh to Peppering High Barn, where you will hit tarmac which soon turns to a minor road. A right turn takes you into Burpham where The Forge & Dragon can be found in a pleasant setting a short way up the hill; then ride on south for Arundel.

Places To Visit:
Arundel Castle (tel: 01903 883136);
Arundel Cathedral (tel: 01903 882297).

Top Pubs:
The Frankland Arms at Washington;
The Forge & Dragon at Burpham;
plenty of pubs and cafes also in Arundel.

Bramber Castle and the Downs

Mainly Offroad

Area: Mid-way along the South Downs, to the north of Worthing and Shoreham.

OS Map: Landranger 198 Brighton and the Downs.

Route:
Bramber Castle CP (GR:185106)
Upper Maudlin Farm (GR:173099)
Steyning Bowl/SDW (GR:162095)
SDW (GR:149111)
Cissbury Ring CP (GR:139083)
Steep Down (GR168079)
Lancing College (GR:195063)
Botolphs/Downs Link (GR:194093)
Beeding Hill/SDW (GR:209095)
Bramber Castle CP (GR:185106)

Nearest BR Stations: Worthing/Lancing.

Approx Length: 19 miles (31km).

Time: Allow 3–4 hours.

Rating: Moderate, but quite energetic with steady ups and downs rewarded by wonderful views.

Bramber Castle is a good place to start; alternatively there are car parks at Cissbury Ring a mile east of Findon, and on the road between Sompting and Steyning, just north of Beggars Bush and at Steyning Bowl.

1. From the Bramber Castle roundabout, follow Maudlin Lane uphill to the south-west, crossing a road and continuing uphill to join a private road/bridleway that leads to open country past Upper Maudlin Farm. From here it's a steady pedal up the hillside on a concrete track, joining the South Downs Way at the top Steyning Bowl.

2. Turn right along the SDW, passing the trig point above Steyning Round Hill and riding in the direction of Chanctonbury Ring which can be seen on the hilltop ahead. After about a mile, turn left on an unmarked bridleway track that leads westwards past some isolated scrubby trees. This joins a track heading due south from Chanctonbury Ring.

3. From here it's a steady, fast ride southwards to Cissbury Ring, though watch for the potholes. Cissbury Ring is a magical place if there's nobody around, but is marred because it is so easily accessible, with the car park nearby. Whatever you do, *don't* ride over the ramparts of this ancient hill fort which suffers mightily from the weight of visitors.

4. Bear left downhill by the side of Cissbury Ring, joining a bridleway track (the signposting here is at first confusing) which heads east past a solitary and rather unlovely storage building. The bridleway crosses a track to the north of Lychpole Farm after some steady up-and-down riding, coming to the Sompting/Steyning back road, about half a mile north of Beggars Bush, by a car park.

5. Ride straight over here, joining a bridleway that leads under overhead powerlines by the side of a steep down. Take the second bridleway

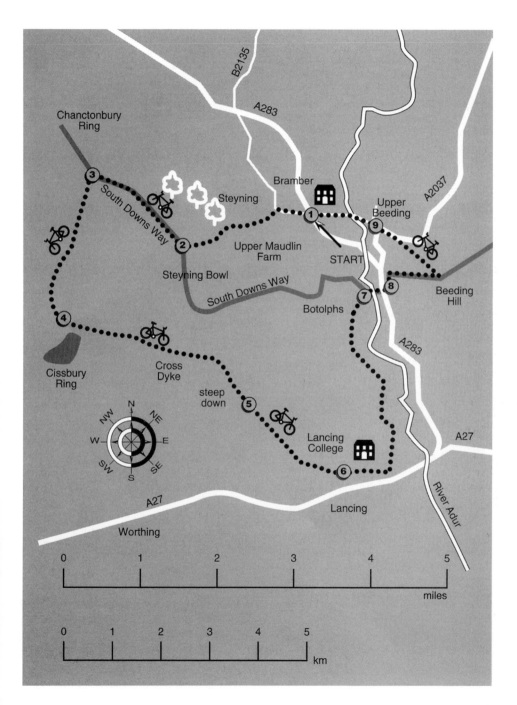

Lancing college looks very fine on the hillside below the downs as the route heads towards the River Adur.

track to the right, following the side of the down south-east towards Lancing. The route is easily followed, but it is narrow in places and you'll find dog-walkers escaping the nearby urban splurge of Shoreham and Worthing.

6. When Lancing College comes into view on the left, the bridleway bears due east to join a road that runs to the south of the college buildings. This emerges close by the noisy, threatening A27, but joins a quiet road that runs north along the west bank of the River Adur to rejoin the SDW at Botolphs. (The Downs Link follows the east side of the River Adur on a hard track, and might provide an alternative route if you can find the way onto it.)

7. Just past the church at Botolphs, turn right to cross the River Adur by the Downs Link noticeboard; this will get you back onto the South Downs Way. Alternatively, if you want to head direct to Bramber Castle you can follow the Link route along the west side of the river.

8. Across the river you come to a handy water tap, and then meet the A283. The SDW is clearly signposted here in both directions, but the traffic is beastly and getting across the A283 is by no means easy. Once across, a narrow and sometimes quite muddy track leads fairly steeply up the hillside, breaking out into open country near the top of Beeding Hill where there is a small car park.

9. From Beeding Hill, a rough track leads north-westwards, down to Castle Town. Follow the signs through Bramber to the castle where this last part of the route features excellent bike-friendly traffic-calming structures. There isalso a variety of pubs to choose from along here, or why not stay in the very pleasant grounds of Bramber Castle for a picnic?

Places To Visit:
Bramber Castle (English Heritage);
Steyning town.

Top Pubs:
The Castle Hotel at Bramber.

The view back to Chanctonbury Ring, heading south of the South Downs Way.

Bramber Castle and the Downs Link

This is a fast ride with a lot of road work, but it is almost all pleasant riding. The climb to the top of the downs gives a nice touch of variety, ready for the descent to Bramber Castle which is well hidden despite its proximity to a large roundabout on the A283 close to the south-eastern fringes of Steyning. There's a small free car park here.

Mainly Offroad

Area: Mid-way along the South Downs, to the north of Worthing.

OS Map: Landranger 198 Brighton and the Downs.

Route:
Bramber Castle car park (GR:185106)
Downs Link
Patridge Green (GR:190190)
Thistleworth Farm (GR: 155189)
Ashurst (GR:179162)
Wiston (GR:144143)
Chanctonbury Ring/SDW (GR:140120)
Steyning Round Hill/SDW (GR:160104)
Bramber Castle car park (GR:185106)

Nearest BR Stations:
Worthing/Lancing.

Approx Length: 23 miles (37km).

Time: Allow 4 hours.

Rating: Mainly easy on level ground with good riding surfaces; one big climb up to the South Downs Way east of Chanctonbury Ring.

1. From Bramber Castle ride downhill towards the roundabout, and immediately turn left on the narrow lane which runs northwards parallel to the main A283. Look out for the Downs Link signs here, and follow them out past the bungalows, joining a hard track which continues north into countryside past Kings Barn Farm.

2. Ride on past the sewage works, crossing the old railway line which unfortunately has been destroyed here. This necessitates a bridleway dog-leg via Greenfields and Wyckham Farm, before turning due east across a field to get back on to the old Downs Link railway line – it can be muddy across here in wet weather.

3. Once on the Downs Link proper, it is mainly fast and easy riding, following the route of the old railway northwards over level ground. A fast, steady speed is possible, but look out for local dog-walkers along the route.

The track crosses the River Adur by Stretham Manor – this is a nice area to stop for a picnic in summer – before coming to Henfield, where it hops off the railway for a few hundred yards. The way is quite well signposted, but as with other sections of the Downs Link it seems a crime that the line wasn't left intact for leisure use when it was closed as a railway.

4. Once beyond Henfield the Downs Link re-crosses the River Adur, reaching Homelands Farm where its track is once again barred by the unlovely sprawl of Partridge Green. The bridleway directs you along a metalled farm drive to join the B2135 road on the southern outskirts of Partridge Green.

Bramber Castle and the Downs Link

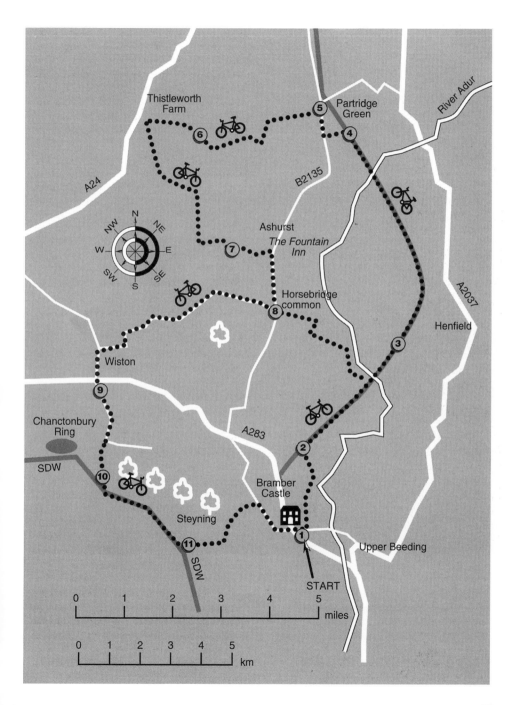

Bridleway signpost on top of the Downs, in thick mist by Chanctonbury Ring. Be prepared for poor weather!

5. Just before the old rail bridge and continuation of the Downs Link, turn off left onto a private road (bridleway) heading due west past orchards on the south side of Partridge Green. Between here and the A24 to the west there are extensive private roads marked as bridleways in farmland surroundings; you may meet the occasional car, but generally it is car-free and flat, which is how a lot of us think cycling should be!

6. Follow the road past Lloyts Farm, crossing another tributary of the River Adur and bearing left to head due south at Lock Farm. The bridleway which continues south here sets off across fields and can be exceptionally muddy as it drops to re-cross yet another River Adur tributary; better to rejoin the private road/bridleway that continues westwards towards Sands Farm. Navigation is pretty easy, but you need to keep an eye on the bridleway signs; on this section I missed a turning and ended up by Hobshort's Farm, off course to the north.

7. Past Sands Farm – a smart and prosperous establishment – the bridleway joins a country lane close to the din of the dual-carriageway A24 about half a mile south of Dial Post. Turn left to go south here, following this fairly quiet road through pleasant woodland and coppices.

Just past Honeybridge Farm you have the choice of staying with the road which swings east towards Ashurst, or trying one of a couple of bridleways which continue due south on either side of King's Barn Farm. Because it was fairly wet and muddy I opted for the former, a decision that was vindicated as Ashurst probably has the nicest pub on the route, even though it is set on a fairly busy road.

8. From the pub at Ashurst, follow the B2135 southwards for about a mile to Horsebridge Common. Here you have a choice: if you want to cut short the ride, turn left onto a bridleway which goes east towards the River Adur, joining the riverside route and then reconnecting with the Downs Link just south of Stretham Manor; if you want to carry on for the South Downs, turn right on the opposite side of the road, following the direction for Wiston.

9. This is another quiet, pleasant road which heads westwards through woodland. At the Wiston T-junction turn left uphill to cross the main A283 by Buncton Farm, joining a narrow dead-end road which heads up the hillside by the Wiston estate. Take the left fork by the estate office, and keep on uphill, passing a car park and then joining a track by Great Barn Farm which leads up to the top of the downs by

the side of Chanctonbury Ring. The track narrows as it heads up through woodland, and although it is possible to ride to the top, you would need a lot of determination and good conditions to manage without some pushing.

10. At the top, the track breaks out of the trees and into the open about half a mile south-east of Chanctonbury Ring, which is well worth a diversion if you haven't already visited it on another ride. Then follow the South Downs Way signpost, and head south-east on a steady downhill in the direction of Steyning Bowl.

11. A number of routes lead down to Bramber from the top of the downs. The easiest and most direct is past the trig point on the right side of the track at the top of Steyning Round Hill, where the next bridleway turning on the left leads eastwards off the South Downs Way.

This unexpectedly joins the road after a short distance – take care here – before heading steeply downhill into Steyning which is a pleasant town worth exploring. From here it is a short ride back to Bramber Castle.

Places To Visit:
Bramber Castle (English Heritage).

Top Pubs:
The Castle Hotel at Bramber;
The Fountain Inn at Ashurst;
also pub stops at Henfield and
Partridge Green.

Bramber Castle to Wolstonbury Hill

You could either start this ride from Bramber Castle, already used for Rides 13 and 14, or from the Devil's Dyke CP on top of the downs above Hove which has the advantage of starting high.

Mainly Offroad

Area: Mid-way along the South Downs, to the north of Shoreham and Brighton.

OS Map: Landranger 198 Brighton and the Downs.

Route:
Bramber Castle CP (GR:185106)
Tottington Barn YHA/SDW (GR:221106)
Devil's Dyke/SDW (GR:258111)
Wolstonbury Hill (GR:285138)
Bedlam Street (GR:278154)
Poynings (GR:265120)
Fulking (GR:248113)
Bramber Castle CP (GR:185106)

Nearest BR Stations: Hassocks.

Approx Length: 23 miles (37km).

Time: Allow 4–5 hours.

Rating: Moderate, but with hard climbs and the potential for extreme mud.

1. From the Bramber Castle CP there are two routes to the top of the downs to join the SDW: either follow the Downs Link south along the west side of the River Arun to the river crossing at Botolphs, joining the SDW on the other side of the A283 and riding up to the top of Beeding Hill; or follow the road along Bramber High Street, crossing the River Arun in the town and then bearing right to join the main A2037. Follow this road eastwards for a few hundred yards, and after the mini roundabout turn right onto the first signposted bridleway track which goes steeply up the hillside to Beeding Hill.

2. From Beeding Hill, the SDW follows a made-up road along the top of the down as far as the YHA Truleigh Hill hostel at Tottington Barn, but few cars come this way and the tarmac soon gives way to a rough surface.

Tottington Barn is a modern hostel in a bleak position (tel: 0903 813419), busy during the summer months but closed for much of the winter. Beyond it the 'road' leads on uphill towards the twin radio masts at the top of Truleigh Hill, passing a few isolated houses beyond Freshcombe Lodge, before following the top of the down on a series of steady ups and downs that lead on past Edburton, Fulking and Perching Hill.

3. The SDW continues due east along the top of the downs, crossing the road that leads to the Devil's Dyke car park with the hilltop pub of that name just beyond. From here it bears northeast round the side of the Dyke, following a narrow path downhill through woodland – watch out for walkers here – that eventually swings steeply down to join the road at Saddlescombe.

4. Cross over and follow the SDW signpost

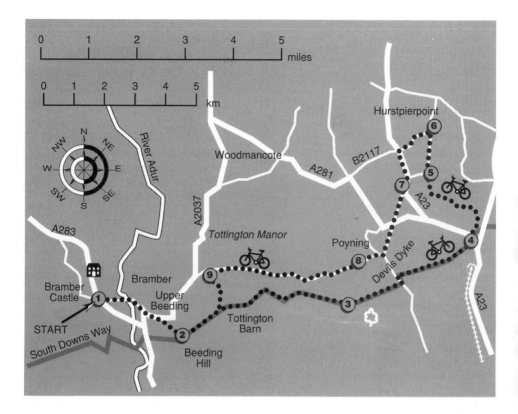

round the back of the farm buildings at Saddlescombe – this seems an unnecessary diversion – bearing left past the last houses on a narrow track that heads up West Hill to the top of the down; you then drop downhill on a hard track to Haresdean by the side of the fast-moving A23 bound for Brighton. An official cycle route leads along the side of the A23 allowing you to cross in reasonable safety; then ride uphill into the hamlet of Pyecombe, unfortunately sandwiched between the A23 and A273.

5. Past the church in Pyecombe, take the next turn on the left by a noticeboard; this is a lane that becomes bridleway heading due north, a rebuilt cinder trail up the side of the hill, with the A273 relatively quiet in the valley below. After half a mile or so, you come to a bridleway

crossroads: turn left here, following the wide track through a gate and up Wolstonbury Hill which is in a fine setting.

6. Bear right round the side of Wolstonbury Hill, following the bridleway round to the north; by this stage it has deteriorated into an indistinct trail, which tends to be badly ripped by horses' hooves and potentially very muddy. The bridleway then drops steeply down the north side of Wolstonbury Hill on a track that is so poor it's likely to be unridable; it heads into a narrow belt of trees, with a straight track leading across the next field to Foxhole Cottages.

This track can also be desperately muddy, and it may be necessary to carry your bike the whole distance. In dry weather it would certainly be a bumpy ride.

7. At Foxhole Cottages, the bridleway joins a pleasant track that heads north through the woods at Randolph's Copse, joining a metalled lane past Randolph's Farm.

Just before Bedlam Street turn left by a bridge, and then left again onto the B2117 heading eastwards. This takes you back across the A23, where you rejoin part of the official cycle way which stretches down its west side. Follow this cycleway south as far as Newtimber Place, where you turn right onto a dead-end lane by the entrance.

8. From Newtimber Place this quiet lane heads south-west towards Poynings, crossing the A281 before heading up and steeply down into Poynings where there is a pleasant pub. The road then continues westwards along the north foot of the downs, passing through Fulking (another pub stop) and on through Edburton bound for Bramber.

9. At Tottington Manor there is a pub/hotel; if you stay on-road from here you have to follow the A2037 for just over a mile to get back to Bramber. If you feel like climbing back to the top of the downs – or are doing a circuit which leaves out Bramber – a bridleway climbs up the hillside on the opposite side of the road to Tottington Manor. It is clearly signposted, but fairly steep and badly eroded in places, and at the top directions become a little difficult to follow. You should come out onto the SDW a few hundred yards south-west of the Tottington Barn YHA, ready to ride back to Bramber or complete the rest of the circuit in the other direction.

Places To Visit:
Bramber Castle (English Heritage);
Devil's Dyke hill fort.

Top Pubs and Other Stops:
The Castle Hotel at Bramber;
Tottington Manor at Edburton;
also pub stops at Upper Beeding, Devil's Dyke, Pyecombe, Poynings, Fulking.

Right: Bramber Castle is a total ruin, but makes a very pleasant place to stop.

The climb to the top of the Downs above Tottington Manor is hard, and the route can be confusing.

Ditchling Beacon and the Downs

Mainly Offroad

Area: The middle of the South Downs
Ditchling Beacon above Brighton.

OS Map: OS Landranger 198
Brighton and the Downs.

Route:
Ditchling Beacon (GR:332132)
South Downs Way (GR:352128)
Blackcap (GR:373125)
Buckland Bank (GR:363110)
St Mary's Farm (GR:348108)
South Downs Way (GR;338128)
Ditchling Beacon (GR:332132)

Nearest BR Station: Hassocks.

Approx Length: 10 miles (16km).

Time: Allow 2–3 hours.

Rating: Moderate. One long climb back
up to Ditchling Beacon; otherwise minor
climbs on chalk, flint, grass or mud.

This is a comparatively short ride within easy reach of Brighton which crams a lot of variety into its short length. It can easily be extended, with an additional loop westwards towards Clayton windmills and the south via the Sussex Border Path to Lower Standean, and starts at the top of the most infamous hill of the London to Brighton bike ride - Ditchling Beacon.

1. The car park at Ditchling Beacon is right on the top of the downs, marked by a National Trust sign. Start off eastwards, but take great care crossing the road on this dangerous bend which motorists appear to regard as a rally stage. Head straight on along the South Downs Way which is clearly marked. Cross over the track heading to Streathill Farm on the right, and continue past the bridleway sign which points to Ashcombe Bottom.

2. Ride past the trig point on your left at Blackcap, and push on up Mount Harry. The going is good and fast on chalk and firm earth, and you soon come to the end of this three-mile section along the South Downs Way.

The turn-off is easily recognizable because the electricity pylon lines run directly overhead as you pass through a gate near the start of a downhill. A few yards further on, turn right down a narrow bridleway that goes into woods; there is a short, muddy section before you break out into open ground by a gate.

3. Go through the gate and head across the field to the next bridleway gate, and the one after; then go left, downhill across a big grass field. You can't see where you are heading because it's hidden by the brow of the hill, but you soon come to the bottom left-hand corner of the field. Watch out! Here the track drops down a short 'bike severe' downhill with a very limited run-out at the end - not recommended for a fast descent!

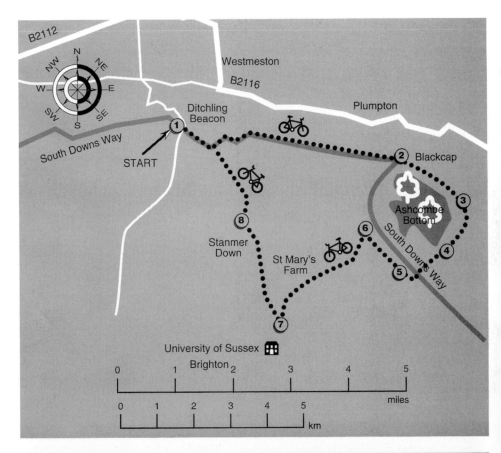

B2112

Westmeston

B2116

Plumpton

Ditchling
Beacon

South Downs Way

START

① ② Blackcap

③

Ashcombe
Bottom

④

⑧

Stanmer
Down

⑥

St Mary's
Farm

South Downs Way

⑤

⑦

University of Sussex

Brighton

0	1	2	3	4	5

miles

0	1	2	3	4	5

km

Many bridleways on the South Downs pass through farmland. Treat the animals you meet with respect, and if in doubt push your bike past them. Don't forget to shut all gates.

Not all tracks are this good when you ride on the Downs above Brighton. When there are no pubs or cafes on the route, be sure to take enough food and drink with you for the duration.

4. At the bottom turn left, and then immediately right through bridleway gates and a sheep pen, heading up the grassy hill and into woods. A short track through the woods leads to another gate, where you cross a field following the bridleway sign, heading along a track which skirts the side of the next field with a hill sloping down to the right.

5. When you come to a bridleway crossing track, head straight over; the correct bridleway route bears right across the field, although on our visit there was no clear indication of this.

Near the bottom right-hand corner you will see the next bridleway gate; go through it, and uphill to the next gate, 200 metres distant.

6. Here, join a track where you turn right, and ride up towards the pylons at Buckland Bank. Just before you reach them, turn hard left onto another bridleway; this takes you south-west along a deeply rutted track with views over St Mary's Farm in the valley.

Carry on for almost a mile, ignoring a bridleway sign to the right and keeping on past a couple of old barns until you reach a tarmac driveway. Here you turn hard right, following the bridleway signs uphill, and then down on tarmac to St Mary's, which is a small and isolated settlement.

7. Just past the farm buildings the track bends round to the right. Take the bridleway sign straight ahead, uphill along the side of a field.

After a long plug upwards the track levels out, and then passes a bridleway gate on the left. Ignore this and carry straight on, going down a narrow, muddy hill to the valley bottom. What comes down must go up, and there follows a short, stiff ride up over grass to a gate.

8. Go through and into a field, pushing on uphill with Ditchling Beacon in sight to the left ahead of you. It's a long climb, but the going is good and eventually you reach a gate where you turn right through a few trees before rejoining the South Downs Way a few yards uphill.

From here, turn left back to the car park where if you are lucky the ice-cream van may be waiting for you; if not, you may find refreshment in nearby Ditchling.

Places To Visit:
Lewes town and castle;
Clayton windmills.

Top Pubs:
None on this route, unless you ride down to Plumpton, where you will find the Half Moon.

Firle Beacon and the Downs

Mainly Offroad

Area: East end of the South Downs Firle Beacon and Alfriston.

OS Map: Landranger 198/199 Brighton and the Downs/Eastbourne and surrounding area.

Route:
West Firle (GR:467075)
South Downs Way CP (GR:468059)
Beddingham Hill (GR:454060)
Gardener's Hill (GR:462031)
Denton Hill (GR:487033)
Alfriston (GR:521033)
South Downs Way (GR:510035)
Bostal Hill (GR:497048)
Firle Beacon (GR:485059)
West Firle (GR:467075)

Nearest BR Station: Glynde.

Approx Length: 14 miles (23km).

Time: Allow 3 hours.

Rating: Moderate. Several climbs, the longest of which is back up from Alfriston. Good going mainly on grass and chalk. Some poor signposting on southern loop.

This ride could start at Alfriston, although the car parking is much easier on the downs above West Firle and psychologically it is always better to start high! It could also be combined with Ride 18 to make a really demanding route for those who can handle it. From the A27, take the road running south to West Firle, bearing left for Firle Beacon. Drive or ride on up to the top of the downs where there is a large, free car parking area to start from.

1. Ride west on the SDW along the top of the down towards the radio masts on a good grass track. A short way on, you will come to a cattle grid with a track coming up from the north and a bridleway sign pointing straight on. However, take the unmarked bridleway down to the left heading south across a field. Go past a barn, continuing downwards, and then at the foot of the hill fork left uphill.

2. Ride up a short way until you reach a field, where you go straight across, following the barely discernible track across to a bridleway gate (no fence); then take the narrow, grassy track between two fields that bends back round to the south and heads down to Gardener's Hill.

The track bears right and then left downhill, and eventually joins with a crossing track in a small valley with a clump of trees beyond. We found no signposting on this section, so careful map-reading may be necessary.

3. Turn left, heading north-east up the crossing track at Gardener's Hill to a bridleway gate. Follow the bridleway left round the edge of the next field, and along a narrow track on its northern edge, still heading north-east.

Go through a gate, then up the side of another field until you reach a gate where the bridleway sign points onwards and to the left. A track joins from the right, and at this point you have come almost two miles from the turning at Gardener's Hill.

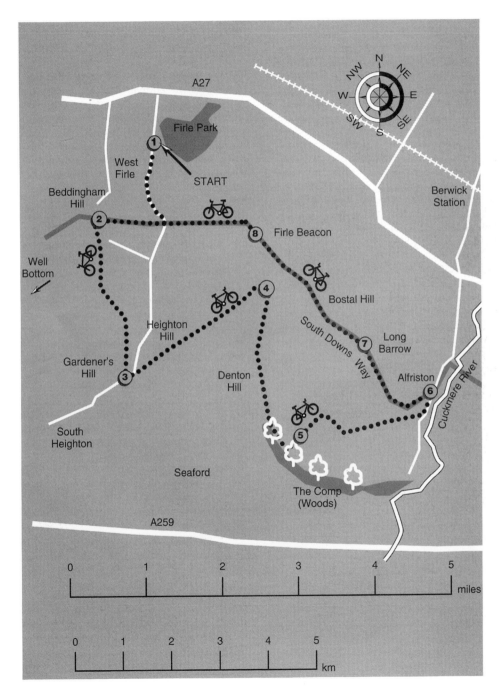

4. Turn right here, and after 100 metres bear left to join the crossing track. Turn right onto it, and head south on a fast surface with fine views over the downs to your left and out over the sea at Seaford ahead.

Go through a gate, ride a short way uphill, and then through another gate. Keep straight on past a bridleway sign to the left, continue keeping left, and then if you want a difficult technical section follow a narrow bridleway track signposted downhill. This track slithers downwards, perilously close to a barbed-wire fence. An alternative, easier route is to ignore this turning and go straight on for The Comp where you can backtrack on another, much wider bridlepath.

5. This is where you ride off Landranger 198 onto 199 – both tracks come down to a valley, where you go through a gate marked with a bridleway blob. Continue uphill, going through the next gate and toiling up the side of a field, turning right along its perimeter at the top at a point marked by a stone.

Go through another gate out of the field, and carry on along a long, fenced track to the left, which swoops down towards Alfriston with wonderful views out over Long Barrow.

6. Eventually you hit a hard track which takes you down into the centre of Alfriston; here there are plenty of pubs, shops, tea houses and souvenirs, and it is likely to be crowded in high summer. It also has a YHA located at Frog Firle (tel: 0323 870423).

Bear right at the tourist sign for the National Trust's Alfriston Clergy House; this brings you out by the church, an attractive place for a picnic. From there, follow the horse track for fifty metres parallel to the river, then turn left, back up into the town; here you can join the South Downs Way for the return trip, either making a longer return trip via Firle, or continuing on Ride 18.

7. To get on to the South Downs Way westwards turn left through Alfriston, and after about twenty-five metres go right onto a road with a South Downs Way sign. When the road forks, bear left up past modern houses; the road becomes a hard track that climbs up gradually to the grassy downs. It's a long pull but not too taxing, and the way is very well signposted. As the view unfolds and you gain height you begin to catch glimpses of the radio masts, egging you on to your destination.

8. Keep on through the few buildings of Bopeep Farm where you go straight ahead through the gates, maybe seeing a few hang-gliders jumping off the hill on the right.

Carry on to the trig point perched on top of the tumuli at Firle Beacon, and take in the magnificent view on all sides; from here it's a short ride to the start car park on top of the downs. Alternatively follow the bridleway that goes north-west downhill, heading for West Firle by the side of the Firle Plantation.

Places To Visit:
Alfriston Clergy House NT
(tel: 01323 870001);
Glynde Place (tel: 01273 858224);
Firle Place (tel: 01273 858335);
Charleston Farmhouse
(tel: 01323 811265).

Top Pubs:
The Star, George and Ship at Alfriston;
The Ram at Firle;
other pubs, cafes, tea houses in Alfriston;

The National Trust's Alfriston Clergy House is well worth a visit in summer. The fourteenth-century Wealden Hall House was the first building to be acquired by the National Trust in 1896. It is half timbered and thatched, and contains a medieval hall and exhibition room, plus a cottage garden. The YHA hostel at Frog Firle is about one mile to the south along the road from here.

Alfriston and the Downs

Mainly Offroad

Area: Eastern end of the South Downs – Alfriston, Friston Forest and East Dean.

OS Map: OS Landranger 199 Eastbourne, Hastings and surrounding area.

Route:
Alfriston (GR:521033)
Windover Hill (GR:545033)
Lullington Heath (GR:539019)
Snap Hill (GR:545005)
Friston (GR:551982)
East Dean (GR:562979)
Long Down (GR:572965)
Warren Hill (GR:589975)
South Downs Way (GR: 550028)
Jevington (GR:562013)
Alfriston (GR:521033)

Nearest BR Station: Berwick.

Approx Length: 18 miles (30km).

Time: Allow 4 hours.

Rating: Moderate. Stiff climb out of Alfriston; other less taxing climbs en route. Mainly good going on chalk and grass; slippery after rain.

The downs looming above Alfriston look forbidding, but this is a fine ride and not too taxing. Allow about four hours, and if this isn't enough the ride can be extended in a number of directions: one obvious way is to follow the bridleway from Jevington to Folkington to Alfriston on the return loop, rather than taking the South Downs Way.

1. From the A27, turn off onto the minor road that runs south through Alfriston and beyond; on the outskirts there is a pay-and-display car park on the left, though a more suitable free car park can be found a little way further on.

From the car park, head back north for about 200 metres, turning right across a bridge and over the river. The bridleway goes straight ahead at a T-junction by the side of a house, but watch out here as this is a very blind bend, and great care should be taken when crossing.

2. Head up the hard track, but take it easy as there is a lot of climbing ahead. It soon breaks out into open country, crossing a minor road and then going on up through a gate with a blue bridleway mark. From here, the hard chalk track snakes up the side of the hill past a strange little building which has sprouted a TV aerial. Go through another gate, and follow the track round to the right, where are fine views over the immense bowl of Tenantry Ground below you.

3. At the top of Windover Hill go through a gate and take the bridleway sign to the right, ignoring the one pointing straight ahead.

Fork right at the next sign, about seventy-five metres further on, and then follow the signs across fast, open fields, heading south-west towards Lullington Heath. Go through the gate next to a brown information sign and onto the heath; carry straight on, following the bridleway signs which are very clear. Fork left for Charlston Bottom which takes you on a long, fast downhill; follow the signs for Snap Hill uphill and down, then another fast hill which leads to a metalled crossing track.

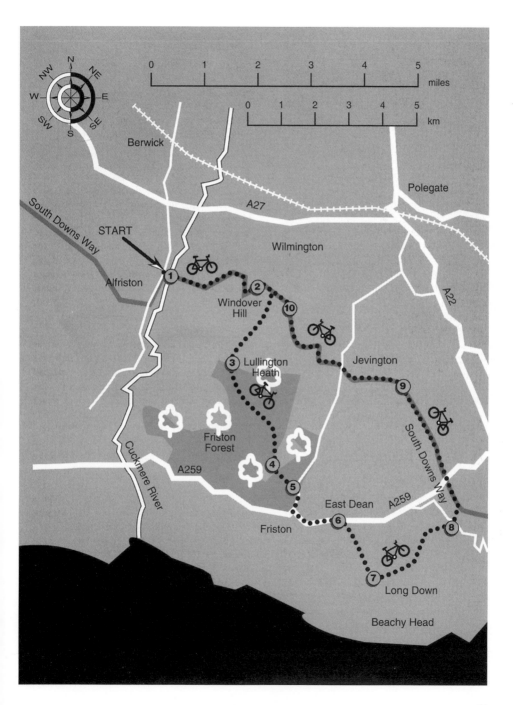

Stop awhile at the fine church green in Alfriston, which is rated as probably the most popular tourist village in Sussex. The church of St. Andrew dates from the fourteenth century and is built on a Saxon barrow.

4. Go straight over here, following the sign for Friston. The going is very good on hard, wide tracks despite the hoofmarks of many horses. Carry straight on, and eventually you break into open ground with some brush fences, horse-race style, to your right. Go down through the trees, ignoring the sign to West Dean and following the sign to Friston straight ahead. Here you join a bridleway which runs up the side of a long, straight lane with Friston Place located over to the right.

5. When you reach the road turn right, and then after about fifty metres left onto a sign-posted bridleway; follow this up a narrow track and across a field to the outskirts of Friston.

Here you could turn left and ride north-east up towards Willingdon Hill, turning left for Jevington; this cuts out the southern section of the route.

6. If you opt to push on, turn right to rejoin the road, and bear left onto the A259. Keep on the A259 downhill past Friston and East Dean, and near the top of the hill on the outskirts of the town turn right onto a bridleway just opposite the Eastbourne Heritage Coast sign.

Follow this track up and down along the side of a field, passing a bridleway sign to the right and taking the sign straight on, marked as bridleway on the OS map.

7. You will come to a barn with wonderful views out over Beachy Head; go through the gate on its right side, and head left on a long downhill by the side of a fence. After a short uphill this brings you to a bridleway crossing track with a house off to the left. Here you follow the bridleway sign straight ahead up the extremely steep grassy hill, bearing left beyond the row of trees to find the next bridleway gate set in the row of trees beyond.

8. Turn left when you reach this gate, following a good track and keeping straight ahead for just over a mile until you hit the road with fine views out past Eastbourne over the sea.

Bear left along the side of the road past Black Robin Farm, and where the B2103 joins it, cross over and head off to the right on a bridleway. Bear left at a junction marked by bridleway and footpath stones, and then left again up to a pond with a couple of benches; here you might like to stop and recuperate a while.

9. Head on until you reach the A259, where you cross straight over onto the South Downs Way. Ride past the golf club and head out into open country, following the South Downs Way on a long downhill which bears down left into Jevington; here you can find a pub, as well as a tea and coffee house.

From the bridleway, go right for a short way along the road, and then bear left up past the church, still on the South Downs Way. This takes you past a corral with some very classy-looking horses, and on up a track which is criss-crossed with tree roots, making this a tricky uphill section.

10. Carry on following the signs for the South Downs Way, turning right onto open country, then bearing left across a large field with a tumulus and a strange garrison-style building over to the right. Continue to follow the South Downs Way signs, and eventually you will join up with your outward route at the top of Windover Hill.

11. Cruise down towards Alfriston, though at the foot of the hill where you join the road just before the bridge, follow the bridleway sign through the gate to the left. Keep along the left side of the field parallel to the river, and you will reach a gate where you turn right.

Directly in front is a small bridge which leads on to White Bridge, taking you across the River Cuckmere into Alfriston. Here you may care to pause awhile on the fine church green, or follow the signs for horses round to the right, turning right when you reach the road which will take you back to the car parks.

Places To Visit:
Alfriston Clergy House NT
(tel: 01323 870001).

Top Pubs:
The Star, George and Ship at Alfriston; also pub and tea house at Jevington.

The North Downs

The North Downs of Surrey offer a relatively compact area of exceptionally hilly country, within easy reach of London, the M25, and surrounding built-up areas. Despite this proximity, it is a fine area in which to get away from it all, and one which is well criss-crossed with many bridleways – in fact it is so well served that it can be easy to get lost! This area is predictably popular with walkers and horse-riders, but with care and consideration they can exist in harmony with mountain bikers, enjoying the range of rides which follow and which can all be strongly recommended.

Ride 19: The Downs Link

Ride 20: The Devil's Punchbowl

Ride 21: Guildford Westwards

Ride 22: Guildford to Leith Hill

Ride 23: Hatchlands and the Downs

Ride 24: Polesden Lacey and the Downs

Ride 25: Box Hill and the Downs

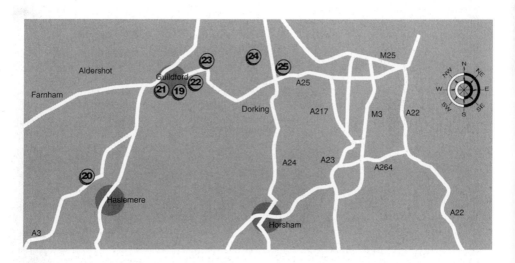

The Downs Link

Mainly Offroad

Area: From Guildford to Shoreham, linking the North Downs to the South Downs.

OS Maps: Landrangers 186/187/198 Aldershot, Guildford and surrounding area/Dorking, Reigate and Crawley/Brighton and The Downs.

Route:
Guildford (GR:993485)
St Martha's Hill (GR:032483)
Bramley (GR:010450)
Cranleigh (GR:060390)
Slinfold (GR:110310)
Southwater (GR:160260)
Patridge Green (GR:19019
Bramber Castle (GR:185106)
Shoreham (GR:213051)

Nearest BR Stations:
Guildford/Horsham (Christ's Hospital)/
Shoreham.

Approx Length: 35 miles (56km).

Time: Allow 4–5 hours.

Rating: Easy. Navigating onto the Downs Link from Guildford requires care, but once on the Link it is all flat riding, although some sections can be muddy and messy after wet weather. Watch out for walkers.

Look out for the special Downs Link signposts.

The Downs Link is a footpath/bridleway which follows the course of an old railway line, linking the North Downs Way at St Martha's Hill in Surrey with the South Downs Way at Steyning in West Sussex, and then continuing south to Shoreham-by-Sea. It covers some 35 miles, using the railway line which Dr Beeching closed in 1966, just over a hundred years after it had been opened. A special railway arch waymarking symbol shows the way, and once you're on the old railway line, navigation is predictably straightforward. However, since this is an end-to-end ride you may need to use British Rail, and for that the city of Guildford makes a convenient start point; or the town of Shoreham, if you prefer to ride south to north, although this has the disadvantage of leaving the most difficult stretch (from the North Downs Way to Guildford) to last.

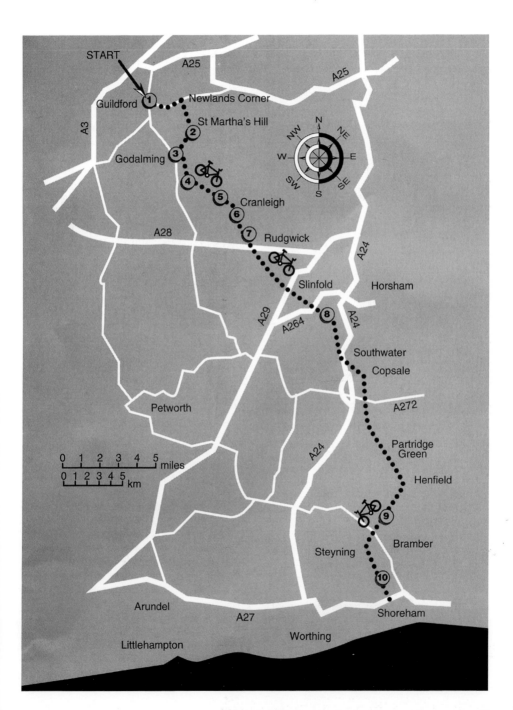

Once you are on the old railway, the Downs Link is easy, good riding all the way.

3. To start with the sandy tracks are a problem. The Downs Link route leads downhill into Tillingbourne valley where it joins a hard track, passing the Lockner Farm riding stables, then crossing the A248. From here it carries straight on, joining another narrow sandy track – a pesky ride – on a gentle uphill by the side of a hedge; it then bears right, wiggling through woods on the edge of Blackheath. This is a big area of heathland and pines where it is important to keep a careful lookout for the railway arch symbols to avoid straying off course.

4. More sandy track riding will bog down your progress, until the route passes Great Tangley Manor on its way to Wonersh Common and Chinthurst Hill; from here there are fine views over the surrounding country. A short way further on and the route reaches the old railway line, dropping down the embankment by a bridge. Turn south (left) here, and it is mainly easy navigation and fast riding all the way to the end of the line, with a few exceptions when the route leaves the old railway, usually because this has been gobbled up by modern developments.

5. Past Bramley, the Wey and Arun Canal runs close to the track; it was originally built to link the Thames with the south coast via the River Wey and River Arun, but was closed when the railways opened in 1868. The track then runs through open country across Run Common, passing an old signal on the way into Cranleigh where the railway disappears for a while. The route bears around the west side of the town (which calls itself the largest village in England), passing the recreation centre and playing fields, and soon brings you back onto the railway.

6. Another forlorn railway signal is passed, and then you come to Baynard's Station which is now privately owned and impeccably restored.

Just past here are the gates of Baynard's Park, with its tree-lined avenue, and then the

1. From Guildford railway station, take the A280 out of town towards Horsham. Past the Yvonne Arnaud Theatre and the River Wey boating centre, take the road turning left just over half a mile from the station; this leads onto the Pilgrim's Way, a signposted trackway up through trees and onto the North Downs Way.

2. The bridleway passes just below the church on St Martha's Hill, close to where the Downs Link officially starts. The church here is in a fine position and worth a visit, but don't ride your bike up to it. Just below the church there is a Downs Link noticeboard by an oddly sited concrete bunker.

bridleway and footpath routes split to divert past a blocked bridge and cutting. Don't take the footpath route which at first seems most obvious, as it goes straight into South Wood where there are stiles and other awkward obstacles. The bridleway route goes left to cross under and over the road bridge, turning into South Wood and rejoining the railway and the footpath a short way further on, across the Surrey/Sussex border.

7. Past Rudwick, the Downs Link crosses the A281 and then goes over the River Arun on a two-tier bridge bound for Slinfold.

Crossing the A29 and A264 it suddenly turns off the railway line by the road bridge, heading along past Weston's Farm to Christ's Hospital where for a short while it runs alongside the modern railway line. The famous public school is set in enormous grounds with playing fields as far as the eye can see.

8. Back on the old railway, the next stop is Southwater where there are more off-railway diversions, crossing the A24 via a handy underpass then continuing along the railway line.

From here on the countryside gets better, with the line passing through the old railway platforms of West Grinstead station. By Partridge Green the route diverts onto the B2135 for a short while, then rejoins the track by Homelands Farm with views of the South Downs opening out ahead. It crosses the River Adur, coming to Henfield where once again it temporarily leaves the track, bearing south-west to cross the River Adur again, this time close by Stretham Manor, and then reaching the outskirts of Bramber at Wyckham Farm.

9. A short road section leads to the A283/A2037 roundabout, close by Bramber Castle (English Heritage) which is well worth a look. The nearby town of Steyning is also worth a visit, with some good buildings and an excellent tea shop in the main street.

From the roundabout the Downs Link route goes south for a while along the side of

You will pass beneath many an old railway bridge along the length of the Downs Link Line.

the busy A283, then leads off to the west to follow the course of the old railway across flat country by the side of the River Adur.

10. At St Botolph's the Downs Link crosses the South Downs Way by the foot/horse/cycle bridge which crosses the River Adur. The Link used to end here, but a new section has been opened using an up-rated footpath which follows the east bank of the River Adur southwards, leading into Old Shoreham from where it is a short ride into Shoreham-by-Sea.

Places To Visit:
Wonersh; Rudgwick;
Southwater Country Park.

Top Pubs:
The Castle Hotel at Bramber;
The Baxcastle at Southwater.

The Devil's Punchbowl

Mainly Offroad

Area: North of Hindhead,
between the North and South Downs.

OS Map: Landranger 186
Aldershot, Guildford and surrounding
area.

Route:
Hindhead Common car park
(GR:892358)
Hankley Common (GR:885415)
Frensham Little Pond (GR:860418)
Tilford (GR:875430)
Elstead (GR:910437)
Ockley Common (GR:915415)
Thursley (GR:902398)
Hindhead Common car park
(GR:892358)

Nearest BR Station: Haslemere.

Approx Length: 18 miles (29km).

Time: Allow 4 hours.

Rating: Moderate. Some of the route is
hard going on sandy tracks; you need to
be careful with navigation.

*The Devil's Punchbowl at Hindhead is a
magnificent open bowl of countryside facing
towards the North Downs. With some very
sandy tracks and a lot of horse-riding it is
possibly not the best mountain biking country, but there are some good sections, fine
views, and the route can be linked with Ride
21 to make a grand day out in the Surrey
countryside.*

1. The NT car park is a short way from the
traffic lights in the centre of Hindhead and
makes a good place to start this ride, though
beware that you can get long tailbacks of angry
motorists both ways along the A3 at peak com-
muting times. To find the bridleway, go past
the cafe and the loos until you come to a track
running along the far west side of the car park.
This leads north along Beacon Hill.

2. This track is easy riding, but there are
plenty of dog-walkers about and there is also a
10mph speed limit sign which you should
abide by. Ignore the track that goes off to the
right and down into the Punchbowl; keep
north by the overhead powerlines – particularly
incongruous in this beautiful area – and follow
the blue bridleway arrows until you enter a
narrow cutting which leads downhill on a difficult surface.

3. This brings you down to a lane between
Hyde Farm and Ridgeway Farm. Keep straight
on ahead, forking right onto another road by
Pitch Place, and then taking the first signposted
bridleway which heads down a narrow track
into the woods on the left. By a solitary house
you then join a fast, wide track on the edge of
MOD land at Houndown. Ride on to the next
crossroads, and turn left to cross Hankley
Common.

4. The bridleway here starts as a tarmac road,
leading past an MOD building; the tarmac then
disappears and sandy tracks take over. Keep on
the main track that continues due west past

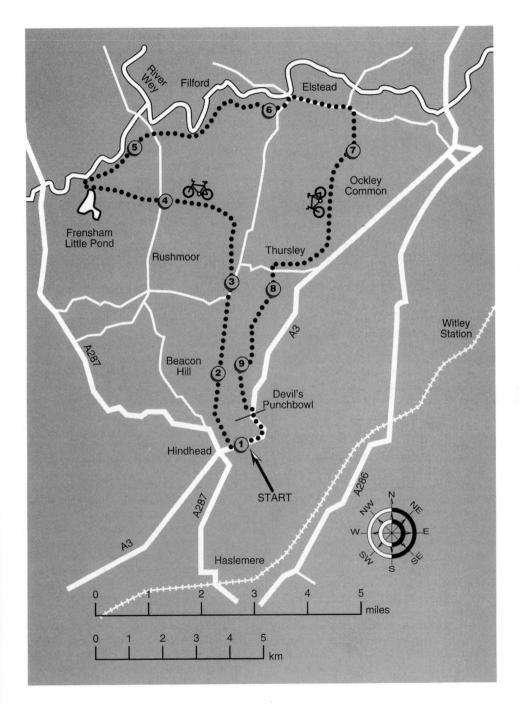

There are 1,400 acres of National Trust heathland and woodland around Hindhead, in an area with a good choice of bridleways.

strange fortifications; the outlook is pleasant here with distant views to the North Downs, but with so much sand there are times when you'll be reduced to pushing.

5. Keep on west past the golf club, and then straight ahead on the road, following it to Frensham Little Pond, an ideal place for a picnic. Just past the car park here, turn sharp right on a bridleway track that leads through the woods, crossing Tilford Common in a northeasterly direction. Once again there is sand, but in general it is pretty good riding to the road at Tilford. (Turn left for a quarter of a mile here to find the excellent pub by the river; they also play cricket on the green.) Follow the bridleway straight ahead, passing Stockbridge Pond and

Hankley Farm on the way to Westbrook with a fine 'Old English' setting by the gate to the big house.

6. Ride out onto the road by the church, turning left to join the B3001 at Elstead. Turn right here, riding eastwards towards Milford; after less than a mile, the first left turn is signposted to Shackleford. *To connect with Ride 21, turn left here and then take the second left fork for The Cider House pub.*

To continue with Ride 20, keep on along the B3001 for another 100 metres or so, and then turn right onto a tarmac lane signposted as a bridleway which heads due south through the light woodland of Royal Common.

7. Carry on riding south, leaving the tarmac to join a variety of tracks that cross Bagmoor and Ockley commons, passing through a forestry landscape that has been partly decimated by tree felling.

Sand and mud will be encountered on the way, but if your navigation is all right you'll eventually come to Hammer Pond close by the side of the A3. Ride on past the pond, which is in a very pleasant setting, and then take the right turning, a track which follows the side of the minor road to Thursley away from the A3.

8. Thursley is a smart, prosperous Surrey village typified by big houses in immaculate condition, and the Range Rover in the driveway; it also has a very pleasant pub. Turn left through the village and continue south, passing the church on a steady uphill which leads past Highfield Farm to join a good track heading up onto Hindhead Common. At the edge of the trees follow this track as it bends round to the right, and then continue south with really magnificent views of the tree-filled Punchbowl opening out as you crest the next hill.

Follow the track over a cattle-grid and past a small house; next on the right is the YHA hostel (tel: 042 860 4285), a delightful place to stay, and with only sixteen beds it is small and friendly by YHA standards.

The view out over the Devil's Punchbowl, a huge spring-eroded sandstone valley, which is known to be one of the largest in Europe.

9. Follow the track up the hill past the Youth Hostel, passing another smart house on the right. From here tarmac takes over, but near the top fork left onto a track which follows the contour line along the side of the Punchbowl, emerging by the busy A3.

Cross the road with great care here, and join the track on the other side which passes beneath an arch designed to limit any vehicles which may decide to drive up here. Keeping right, this track follows the road back to Hindhead, but it is sufficiently far away and high enough to escape most of the noise of the traffic; it also offers some fine final views over the Devils' Punchbowl before you reach the side of the A3 once again, right opposite the main exit to the car park. Then it is just a matter of seeing how long it takes for a motorist to 'allow' you to cross the road.

Places To Visit:
Devil's Punchbowl Nature Trail;
Frensham Little Pond.

Top Pubs
The Barley Mow at Tilford;
The Three Horseshoes at Thursley.

Guildford and the Downs Westwards

Mainly Offroad

Area: The North Downs, west of Guildford.

OS Map: Outdoor Leisure 186 Aldershot, Guildford and surrounding area.

Route:
Guildford (GR:993493)
Sunnydown (GR:967486)
North Downs Way (GR:967479)
Hampton Park (GR:910468)
Shackleford (GR:934455)
Compton (GR:964467)
North Downs Way
Guildford (GR:993493)

Nearest BR Station: Guildford.

Approx Length: 17 miles (27km).

Time: Allow 3 hours.

Rating: Moderate. Mainly straightforward navigation and easy riding with a few ups and downs.

This ride follows the North Downs Way to the west of Guildford, and then takes a southerly loop through the affluent Surrey countryside to complete the circuit. It is mainly pleasant riding, though a few tracks are marred by heavy sand. How long you take to complete the ride may depend on how many pubs you decide to stop at because there are some excellent ones along the way. The route can also be combined with Ride 20, making a grand, full day's figure-of-eight tour that includes the Devil's Punchbowl.

1. If you arrive by train, Guildford makes an excellent place to start the ride from. If you arrive by car there are various options along the way; probably the best alternative start point is the car park at Warren Pond (GR:911458) by Hampton Park at the western end of the route.

2. From Guildford station find your way onto the A3100 for Godalming. Just south of the roundabout, turn right into The Mount opposite St Nicholas Church; this is a steep lane which leads up to the ancient Trackway, taking you due west out of Guildford on a traffic-free lane with views over the Cathedral, which personally I find most unattractive.

Follow the Trackway out onto the road at Sunnydown, keeping left before turning straight down the hillside on a bridleway track which crosses the North Downs Way.

3. Follow the North Downs Way westwards. It is clearly signposted, and is mainly easy riding through woodland and open countryside.

It passes under the A3 and then crosses Puttenham Heath and its golf course, coming to the road at Puttenham below the Hog's Back; here it jigs right and left and then continues westwards through this pleasant village. Try stopping at The Good Intent, which is an inviting pub to visit.

4. At the top of Puttenham village bear left on a narrow lane - the North Downs Way signpost

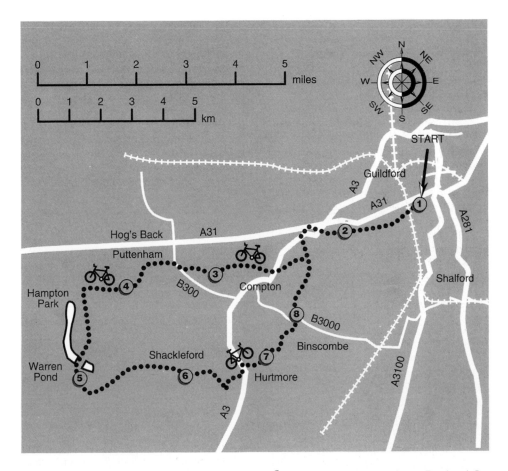

is easily missed here – and continue past Lascombe House over the wilds of Puttenham Common. Here the LDP crosses a lane leading down to Hampton Park and continues westwards as footpath; instead follow the bridleway south along the edge of Puttenham Common, coming up to the 'Fort' at the top of the hill.

Here there is a seat cut from a tree stump, right in the middle of nowhere, with magnificent views to the South Downs. Continue straight on south down the hillside here, turning right before the road to reach the car park by Warren Pond; this is a pretty place, but likely to be very popular with walkers so be very careful how and where you ride.

5. Turn right between Warren Pond and Cut Mill Pond, and then left (south-east) at the crossroads, following the road as it bears round to the east. Just past a couple of houses at Gatwick, take the bridleway track on the left which will take you right through to the road on the outskirts of Shackleford. This is an attractive route and fine for horses, but with half a beachful of sand on the track much of it is very heavy going with a bike.

6. Follow the road into Shackleford: this is a pleasant village, and The Cider House pub is certainly worth a visit. From here, take the road to Hurtmore, forking left onto a bridleway which first follows the edge of the fields, then turns right through trees to cut the corner, rejoining the road and crossing under the A3.

7. Ride up the hill through Hurtmore, ignoring the narrow turning on the left; then look out for an extra-narrow bridleway track which heads north-east across the next road, to join the B3000 a short way to the south-east of Compton. This track starts well, passing a few very smart houses and then running along the side of woodland on a hard cinder surface. It then dives down the hillside – very narrow and overgrown – and crosses a ploughed field (at least it was when I rode it!) where a signpost wouldn't go amiss to help you find the way to the road by the Grange.

8. Cross straight over the B3000 here, riding down a dead-end lane past The Withies pub and on past Polsted Manor, and joining a bridleway that heads north to the North Downs

> **Places To Visit:**
> Loseley Park (Tel: 01483 304440).
>
> **Top Pubs:**
> The Cider House at Shackleford;
> The Good Intent at Puttenham;
> The Withies at Compton;
> also pub stops at Hurtmore
> and Guildford.

Way crossroads below Sunnydown.

From here you can either retrace your wheeltracks along the Trackway; or turn right along the North Downs Way, and follow it due east to join the A281 south of Guildford. This is a pleasant alternative route, winding through woodland before joining Sandy Lane for a fast downhill towards The Ship pub which is at the bottom on the A281.

The view from the North Downs Way southwards is typical of this area, being rural but decidedly affluent.

Guildford to Leith Hill

Mainly Offroad

Area: Due south of the North Downs, between Guilford and Dorking.

OS Maps: Landrangers 186/187 Aldershot, Guildford and surrounding area/Dorking, Reigate and Crawley.

Route:
Guildford (GR:993485)
Newlands Corner (GR:044492)
Hackhurst Downs/NDW (GR:101491)
Park Farm (GR:120483)
Westcott (GR:134486)
Abinger Forest (GR:145455)
Coldharbour (GR:150440)
Leith Hill (GR:140432)
Coverwood (GR:098432)
Pitch Hill (GR:080424)
Winterfold Heath (GR:067427)
Farley Green (GR:060455)
Blackheath (GR:036462)
St Martha's Hill (GR:032483)
Newlands Corner (GR:044492)
Guildford (GR:993485)

Nearest BR Stations: Guildford/Gomshall/Holmwood.

Approx Length: 31 miles (50km), plus 3.75 miles (6km) each way to Guildford BR Station.

Time: Allow 4–6 hours, with time for pub stops and getting lost.

Rating: Moderate. An easy ride, with some tricky navigation and occasional patches of sand.

This is an excellent ride, prowling round the prosperous countryside of southern England where the houses are immaculately tucked away. Some of the tracks are sandy so much so that they look as if the beach has been dumped on them and while the first part of this ride is easily navigated with tracks that are straight and few, from Coldharbour back to St Martha's things get more confusing. There is a maze of tracks in this area, mainly going through woods with basic bridleway signposting.

Getting lost is easy, and an OS map and compass will almost certainly be needed. But even if you get lost, it doesn't necessarily matter – the tracks are mainly great, and it's very good territory for offroad biking, with friendly enough horse-riders.

1. You can start this ride from Guildford BR Station. Find your way up the High Street, and then turn off to the right near the top to go steeply uphill (south-east) by the castle. This will bring you onto the Trackway, an ancient offroad 'road' which runs west-east along the top of Pewley Down to Newlands Corner, passing through fine open countryside.

Newlands Corner has a large car park close by the A25 at the top of Albury Downs, which makes it a good alternative start/finish point.

2. At Newlands Corner cross the road at the top of the hill, and follow the North Downs Way straight ahead due east along an excellent cinder track. The North Downs Way is clearly signposted and mostly easy to follow.

At the first road crossing go straight ahead, and then when you hit the road again (very quiet and very minor) follow it straight on for about half a mile, looking out for a bridleway track going to the right on a left-hand bend. Turn down this track, forking left for the North Downs Way and carrying straight on; a little further on, a more minor track forks left off the main track. Take this route, following the North Downs Way eastwards along Netley Heath.

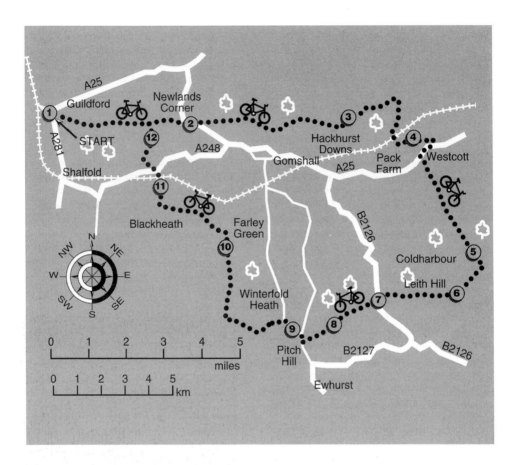

3. You will pass Hackhurst Downs on the right and carry on eastwards. From here, some of the track becomes deeply rutted as it passes through trees; there is a better secondary track running alongside which makes the going easier, although it becomes confusing at times.

Keep on ahead in a more north-easterly direction until you come to a minor road running north to south just before White Downs. Turn right down here, and follow the road on a steep downhill which takes you over the railway line at the bottom of the downs. A short way on there is a bridleway indicated on the left; turn down here, and follow the track round the side of a field towards Park Farm.

4. The track continues east, eventually bringing you to the road by a cluster of houses on the outskirts of Westcott Heath. Here you turn right, and then left onto the A25 for a short distance. Cross the bridge over Pip Brook, and immediately turn right off the A25 onto a track that heads south, following the brook and its ponds by The Rookery where there are a number of attractive houses.

Once past these, the track starts to head uphill with fields on the left, finally coming out into the open with Sylvanus Wood on the left, a big field on the right, and Coast Hill Farm a little way off. Follow the track southwards along the side of the woods; again, there is a secondary track in places, replacing the main track which is deeply sunken and could be incredibly muddy in wet weather.

The track continues in the same direction on a more or less good surface, though a little pushing may be necessary on the way through Abinger Forest in places where there is sand.

5. The track heads downhill along the side of Coldharbour Common towards the hamlet of Coldharbour, where the very accomodating pub awaits you. After the pub, make your way to Leith Hill Tower (NT), a splendid landmark on the hillside at 295m, which on a clear day gives formidable views to the south. Predictably this is a route which is very popular with walkers, and with some steep offroad hills close by, it is important to keep your speed down.

6. To get to the tower, take the track from the pub that goes up the side of the hill, taking the right fork which brings you up to a clearing with a splendidly situated cricket green; on Saturdays in summer you'll more than likely be able to stop and watch a cricket match. Take the left fork past the cricket ground, and then head straight on through the woods, navigating towards the tower.

In this part of Wotton Common there are tracks all over the place and it's easy to take wrong turnings, but keep on in the same ESE direction and you will soon pick up signposts with a conspicuous tower motif. Take care that you don't stray onto footpaths, and be prepared for walkers.

7. Leith Hill Tower has a small kiosk selling drinks and snacks, and is a good place to stop and contemplate and plan the rest of the route.

Going west from here there are countless bridleway tracks in very ridable country, with plenty of ups and downs, and trees and woods all over the place. There is, however, no direct cross-country route, and all you can do is zig-zag in approximatly the right direction. The route which follows gives a pleasant ride.

8. From Leith Hill Tower take the track due west that leads down to the road. Cross straight over, following the bridleway sign towards Burnhouse Copse, and then at the next bridleway sign turn right; this takes you along a track more or less parallel to the road. Look out for the second left turning by High Ashes Farm, and then follow the track all the way westwards towards Holmbury St Mary; this is a good ride, mainly downhill through the woods towards Bulmer Farm. A short uphill brings you back to the road where you turn left; then turn right onto the B2126 through Holmbury St Mary.

9. Holmbury St Mary is an attractive village with two pubs; turn left at the village green by the second one, following the dead-end lane past a few houses and then heading into open country following the same direction. The track

Close encounters with another biker on Leith Hill.

The Leith Hill Tower marks the highest point in south-east England and was built in the eighteenth century. In summer it's worth the climb to the top, which takes you 1,029ft (313m) above sea level.

leads up to a five-way crossroads. Bear right here and carry on in more or less the same direction, following the wide, fast, hard track ahead past Holmbury Hill until it brings you to a small car park by the roadside just south of Coverwood. Turn left downhill on the road, taking the right fork for Ewhurst; a short way on, look for a bridletrack that goes off to the right by the side of Radnor House at the edge of the woods. This is another good ride, going through more open country and finally coming to the road by Cornhill Manor, which is to the north of Ewhurst.

10. Turn right here, following the left fork for about three-quarters of a mile until you come to a pub by the side of Pitch Hill; this is a good place to stop as the pub is in a pleasant position with a big garden and pond in the front.

Suitably refreshed, turn left down a bridleway past the side of Hurtwood Edge, passing a few smart houses. This track soon leads out to the road again, where you turn right for a stiff uphill heading north. The road levels out by a left-hand turning, and here there is a bridleway going more or less straight ahead north across Winterfold Heath and into Winterfold Wood.

11. This is mainly fast riding, leading on to Farley Green. Ride into the village, and then head west for a short distance on-road before forking off onto a bridleway that heads north-west across Blackheath. Some of it is sandy and some is good going, and with tracks and blue bridleway marks all over the place navigation is none too easy, but if you bear west it should eventually bring you out to a car park a short way to the east of the village of Blackheath.

Here you turn right along a dead-end lane, to ride northwards and join the Downs Link which at this point runs down a narrow track by the side of a house.

12. Head northwards on the Downs Link, pushing and riding along the incredibly sandy track towards Lockner Lodge where you cross the modern railway line. From here the track goes straight ahead over the A248 and past Lockner Farm, bearing left downhill and then coming up to a sign for the Downs Link; turn right here to start a steady plod uphill towards St Martha's – the track becomes sandy and unridable near the top, and eventually you reach the end of the Downs Link by a notice-board next to an old concrete pillbox.

Turn right a short way up the hill (carry on up the hill to the left if you want to see the church on the top, but walk), and then take the bridleway track which bears right downhill through the woods to join a minor road below the North Downs by White Lane Farm.

13. Ride uphill keeping north, following the road round to the east at the top of Albury Downs. A little further on, a bridleway (the alternative North Downs Way) runs along the side of the road by the hilltop viewpoint: this is

In summer this is an excellent route for *al fresco* pubs.

the 'Trackway' along the top of the downs, a fast track on level ground which will take you eastwards to Newlands Corner, or westwards to Guildford, in record time.

Places To Visit:
St Martha's Hill;
Leith Hill Tower NT
(tel: 01306 712434).

Top Pubs:
The Plough at Coldharbour;
The Queen's Head at Holmbury St Mary.

Hatchlands and the Downs

Mainly Offroad

Area: The North Downs, between Guildford and Dorking.

OS Map: Landranger 187 Dorking, Reigate and Crawley (for Guildford connection use Landranger 186 - Aldershot, Guildford and surrounding area.)

Route:
Hatchlands/East Clandon (GR:062518)
West Horsley (GR:091527)
King's Hills (GR:097502)
Dogkennel Green (GR:121500)
Park Farm (GR:121483)
North Downs Way/Hackhurst Downs (GR:101491)
Combe Bottom (GR:071491)
Hook Wood (GR:078507)
Hatchlands/East Clandon (GR:062518)

Nearest BR Stations:
Gomshall/Guildford.

Approx Length: 18 miles (29km).

Time: Allow 3–4 hours.

Rating: Moderate. Navigation can be confusing on the North Downs; there can be plenty of mud; and there are a few hills to climb. Much of the distance is offroad.

This is an excellent ride, with the bonus of visiting Hatchlands Park (National Trust) between East Clandon and West Horsley just off the A246. Hatchlands has the usual NT attractions, including a cafe/restaurant; and if you are a music lover you will be pleased to find it also houses Chopin's piano.

1. Hatchlands makes a good place to start/finish the ride if you are planning a visit there. Alternatively there are several parking places en route clearly shown on the OS map. If you prefer to arrive by train you can cycle from nearby Gomshall, or from Guildford which is just over five bridleway miles away along the North Downs Way from the south-west corner of the route at Coombe Bottom.

2. From Hatchlands turn right past East Clandon church, heading due north away from the A246. A narrow country road leads through quiet, flat countryside between Northcote Wood and Gason Wood, crossing the main Guildford railway line where there is a bridleway turn-off which you may like to try, and passing an HM prison in an unlikely setting, surrounded by a huge, white mesh fence.

3. Just past the prison look for a bridleway turning on the right by Sussex Farm. Follow this concrete track eastwards across flat farmland, reaching the road by Jury Farm.
Turn left on the road here, and after a short distance turn right at the next bridleway signpost, following a rougher track eastwards to the next road.

4. Turn right on the road close by Manor Farm, cycling south towards where the downs loom ahead. At the next road junction on the outskirts of Horsley, turn left and then almost immediately right onto a bridleway to continue heading south. This track leads across the railway, through woodland and open fields, to emerge on the A246 just east of West Horsley.

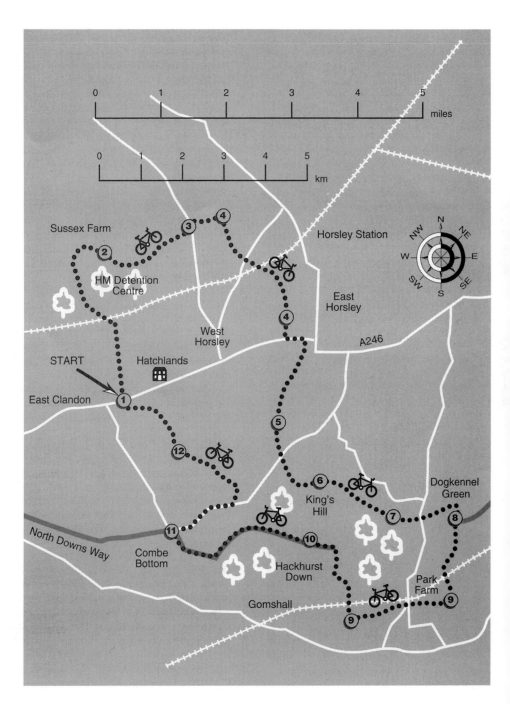

5. Turn left along the main road here; the pavement is easily ridable if you prefer to keep clear of the cars. Cross the A246 at the next bridleway sign which points right into woodland, and continue riding south. The track leads through light woodland, climbing up the side of the downs by The Sheepleas. There are plenty of bridleway arrows, but there is also a confusing mass of tracks, and navigation can be tricky! If you keep straight on, you should come to the next road by Hillside Farm.

6. Follow the track straight over, going quite steeply up a gulley which leads up through Mountain Wood. There are some steep ups and downs ahead, with the track eventually leading down to the road by a sawmill below Netley Heath. Carry on due east here, following the wide track ahead and up through woodland on King's Hill, passing under an unlikely bridge by an isolated, pleasant looking house.

An old monument to a fallen rider marks the way beneath Hackhurst Downs.

7. From here, the track runs along the north edge of the downland woods, passing a few more houses north of Oaken Grove, with a mass of tracks leading on through fine beech woods to the road. It's all very pretty, but after wet weather you will find the most enormous pools and wallowing mud.

You can miss this offroad section by following a tarmac lane north to another road; then turn right to ride eastwards past The Ranmore Arms pub and the next-door cafe.

8. Dogkennel Green is about half a mile to the north-east, via road or bridleway. From here a bridleway track goes due south across White Down, dropping steeply but ridably down the hillside to cross the railway, from where it continues to Park Farm.

Turn right here, and follow the narrow, slightly sandy track along the side of Deerleap Woods on the south side of the valley.

9. This brings you out to the road by Leasers Barn, which is near to a convenient car park (GR:112480); this is a good alternative start place for the ride. *If you are desperate for a pub at this stage, follow the road due south for a mile and a half to Sutton Abinger, where you will find The Volunteer in a very pleasant setting; the Holmbury St Mary YHA is also close by, and excellent for cyclists.*

To continue from Leaser's Barn, follow the bridleway westwards along the south side of the railway, turning right to cross the line after about half a mile. From here, the track leads up the hillside to join the North Downs Way at the top of Hackhurst Downs.

10. Turn onto the North Downs Way which follows a hard track westwards; fine for fast riding, but with walkers and horse-riders about cyclists must take care. Follow this hard track all the way along the NDW to the stables at Hollisten Farm. Turn right here with the acorn/NDW sign, and continue along a narrow track that emerges on the road just above Combe Bottom.

11. Here you leave the North Downs Way *(unless you're bound for Guildford)*, turning right to head north-east along the road.

The first bridleway going north was in a desperately muddy condition the last time I attempted to ride it; if that is the case, take the next left turn down Fullers Lane, joining the bridleway by Hook Wood and following it north-west to Fullers Farm where it splits into two arms turning left and right.

12. Both these tracks go in the right direction. The southern track gets there first, but gives a bumpy ride (past a 'travellers' camp when I rode by) to Blake's Lane Farm. From here, follow the lane westwards to East Clandon, crossing straight over the A246 less than half a mile from the main visitor entrance to Hatchlands.

Hatchlands, a National Trust stately home in a fine setting. It was built in the mid-eighteenth century for Admiral Boscawen, and has interiors by Robert Adam as well as housing the Cobbe collection of keyboard instruments. The garden is by Repton and Gertrude Jekyll.

Places To Visit:
Hatchlands NT (tel: 01483 222482).

Top Pubs (off-route):
The Volunteer at Sutton Abinger
(GR: 105459);
The Ranmore Arms at Dunley Hill
(GR: 113502).

Polesden Lacey and the Downs

Mainly Offroad

Area: The North Downs, west of Dorking.

OS Map: Landranger 187 Dorking, Reigate and Crawley.

Route:
Polesden Lacey (GR:135523)
Stockman's Coomb Farm (GR:128490)
Leasers Barn (GR112482)
Sutton Abinger (GR:105459)
Holmbury Hill (GR:103430)
Friday Street (GR:137457)
Chadhurst Farm (GR:152470)
Ranmore Common (GR:147505)
Polesden Lacey (GR:135523)

Nearest BR Stations:
Dorking/Westhumble.

Approx Length: 25 miles (40km).

Time: Allow 4–5 hours.

Rating: Moderate. There are a few hills and there can be mud; navigation requires care.

This makes an ideal companion ride to the 'Hatchlands and the Downs' circuit (Ride 23), and it too features a famous National Trust house. In fact Polesden Lacey is in a class apart as far as NT properties go, most beautifully situated on the side of a valley; it also has a cafe, with outside seating that will even serve muddy bikers. Once again there are many possible start points for the ride: Polesden Lacey if you plan to visit the house; a half dozen or so car parks along the route; or ride in from Dorking BR station, which is little more than a mile distant from Ranmore Common.

1. From the main entrance to Polesden Lacey, turn sharp left down a track (unmarked bridleway) which leads south, going downhill beneath a quaint thatched bridge, and then more steeply down a track with fine views of the Polesden Lacey valley. Ride up the other side to Yewtree Farm, and then follow the bridleway south to the road which is on the west side of Ranmore Common.

2. Turn right here for a short distance, and then left down a track that goes into woodland (unmarked bridleway); a little further on bear right steeply down the hillside.

Near the bottom join a bridleway track following the contour line westwards on White Downs; keep along here until the bridleway turns south-east through a gate, heading across a field and under the railway, and then coming to Stockman's Coomb Farm.

3. Follow the track ahead, and then take the right turn track (fast, easy riding here) that heads westwards past Park Farm and onto the road at Leasers Barn. This follows the route of Ride 23 for a short distance; here the two rides could be amalgamated into a huge loop for the fit and ambitious rider!

4. From Leasers Barn, follow the road south across the A25 to Sutton Abinger, here you will

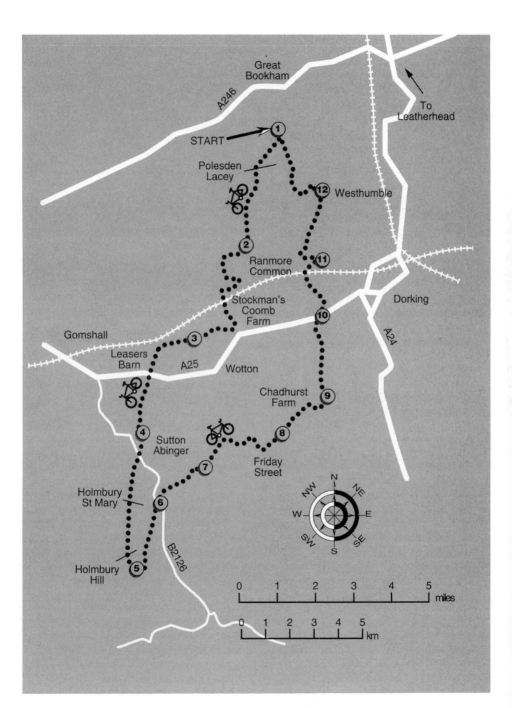

Polesden Lacey was an 1820's Regency villa, remodelled with no expense spared in the early nineteenth century. The huge grounds include decorative features such as this bridge on the south side (below).

find The Volunteer public house. After a pause for refreshment ride south on the B2126 for a short distance, forking right uphill at the YHA sign which brings you up to the Holmbury St Mary Youth Hostel (tel: 0306 730777). This can be recommended as an excellent place to stay, very prettily situated with good facilities, and a lock-up for expensive bikes.

5. Finding the way to Holmbury Hill – with its promise of a huge view over this part of southern England – is not easy. On the map it's almost due south of the Holmbury St Mary hostel, but there is an absolute maze of tracks leading through this extensive area of woodland, and without a compass it is very easy to go off course. The recommended route is to follow the overhead powerlines for some distance, and then edge westwards – but you'll still need good luck to find Holmbury Hill!

6. From Holmbury Hill ride down to the road, and follow it north back to the village of Holmbury St Mary where there is another pub. Turn right for a short distance on the B2126 here, taking the first left turn, and then turning

off at the next bend on a bridleway which heads south-east at Pasture Wood. This is an attractive up-and-down track through woodland, breaking out into the open and reaching another road by High Ashes Farm.

7. From High Ashes Farm turn left onto the road, and then fork right along the side of Wotton Common. After about half a mile, look out for a track entering the woods on the right just opposite a large, isolated house; it leads down to a good track following the valley bottom; keep on downhill, away from the 'Private No Ramblers' sign at the top of a rather smart driveway, and down to the hamlet of Friday Street where you are more than likely to encounter horse riders.

8. By the phone box turn right along a bridle-way track, and then take the first track on the left which leads downhill. Follow it between two pretty little houses, heading uphill and breaking out into the open at Squire's Great Wood; here some up-and-downing will eventually bring you out to Squire's Farm, a prosperous looking establishment. From here, follow the farm drive straight down to the road.

9. Turn right at the road, and then after a short uphill, bear left on a rough bridleway which leads steeply down to Chadhurst Farm (a fine building) and its duckpond. Bear round the left side of the farmstead, joining a track that runs along the side of fields due north towards the downs. Some of the going here can be very muddy, but the track improves as it passes through an area of ponds and fisheries on the outskirts of Westcott. Where the track comes to a gate between two well-kept houses, take the right turn bridleway across Milton Heath; this leads down to the A25.

10. Cross straight over the A25, joining a private road (bridleway) that heads north to Milton Court. Bear left onto a rough track by the mill house, following this across the railway line to the foot of the downs below Ranmore Common. Here the bridleway goes steeply up the hillside on a narrow track up to the road.

(A much more inviting forest 'road' zig-zags up the hillside, but comes to a locked gate on the edge of the Denbies Vineyard with a big 'PRIVATE' sign – this is annoying, as the gate is a stone's throw from the road you want.)

11. Ride on up the road, heading westwards to the top of the down, and turn right onto Ranmore Common. Opposite the magnificent Victorian church, a bridleway track heads north across the common by the side of a very attractive flint-built house. Follow this track down through woodland toward Bagden Farm, taking the left hand track signposted to the remote Tanner's Hatch YHA (tel: 01372 452528).

The fine Victorian church shows the way at Ranmore Common.

12. At the next bridleway T-junction, turn north away from Tanner's Hatch, following a track which heads steadily uphill, passing under a magnificent decorative bridge in the middle of nowhere. This track follows the east side of the grounds of Polesden Lacey, and parts of it become desperately churned up by horses' hooves in wet weather. Nevertheless it is pleasant walking or riding when it is dry, and it soon brings you to the driveway which leads directly into Polesden Lacey. This is an excellent place to finish the ride, where you will no doubt get some bemused looks eating your tea in biker's gear amongst those more smartly attired.

Places To Visit:
Polesden Lacey NT
(tel: 01372 485203).

Top Pubs:
The Volunteer at Sutton Abinger;
The Queen's Head at
Holmbury St Mary.

Box Hill and the Downs

Box Hill Country Park (NT) is potentially very crowded, and the small area of steep hillside that it occupies is best avoided by mountain bikers. The downland to the north-east is much more bike-friendly and has some excellent tracks, though possibly more than with any other route in this book it is best to avoid weekends if possible, and make a point of slowing right down for all horses and walkers. Having said that, I rode it on a perfect May weekday and spent three enjoyable hours during which I met no more than three horse riders, one other mountain biker, and a handful of dog walkers. When it is that quiet, it's a delightful area to go riding.

1. There's a very busy car park on the A24 at Burford Bridge by Westhumble, close to the foot of Box Hill Country Park. If you arrive by car it's a good place to start the ride, though be warned that it is not the most peaceful spot and one imagines it could fill up very easily.

Alternatively you can take the train to the Box Hill station at Westhumble, ride past The Stepping Stones pub and turn left along the side of the A24, until you can cross to the Burford Bridge car park via the roundabout.

2. Ride due north up the hill for Mickleham, soon leaving the roar of the A24 behind. Ride on past the first turning on the right, which zig-zags up to the NT centre at the Country Park.

Take the next right turn for Headley, and almost immediately turn left up a steep, rough track by the side of Juniper Hall Field Centre on the corner.

3. You are now offroad, and very pleasant it is, too. After a rough start, the track smooths out and levels out, bearing round to the right to head north-east across Mickleham Downs.

Ignore turnings off to either side until you are past the trig point at 142m; here the track makes an obvious turn to the left, and then to the right again, to continue in the same direc-

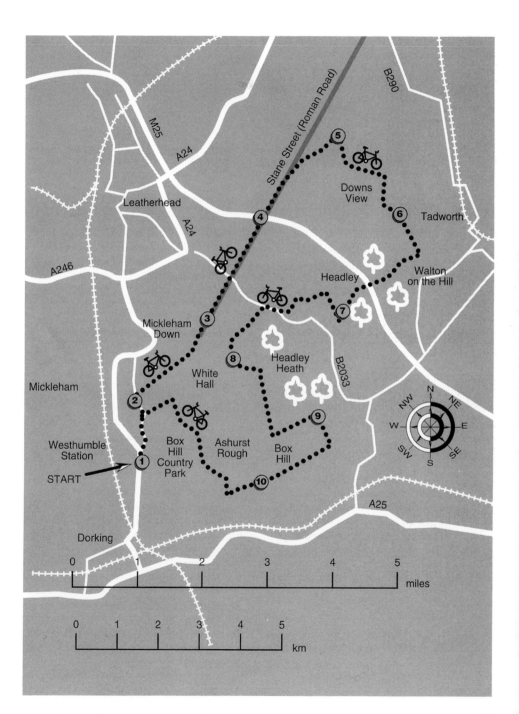

The final offroad section down Lodge Hill, among the thousand acres of woods and chalk downlands of Box Hill.

tion. Ride on straight over the B2033, passing the golf club and probably hitting the first muddy section of the route as you head into Tyrrell's Wood.

4. At the next minor road crossing you have a choice. Either push on across the M25 for a loop south of the Epsom Downs, or cut the ride short by turning right along the road towards Headley. The Epsom Downs can be recommended if you want to get to know a bigger area; apart from being a little urban, the main drawback is that after prolonged wet weather some of the tracks north of the M25 gets churned into a muddy, horse-hooved mess.

5. For the Epsom Downs loop the track continues dead straight, being a part of Stane Street, the old Roman road which is also encountered in the South Downs in Ride 11. However, the Romans would have been amazed to find their fine road crossing the M25 – that piece of modern history which has destroyed so much fine countryside – but thankfully its din is soon left behind as the track continues, past the equestrian centre at Thirty Acre Barn.

Here you hit tarmac after a long and satisfying section offroad. Keep straight ahead at the next crossroads, and then at the bottom of the valley turn right onto the bridleway which starts as a tarmac lane leading to the farm. *Alternatively you could ride on up to the racecourse, but the downland here is better suited to horses than bikes and there are a lot of cars about.* Follow the bridleway up by the side of the farm, joining an unpleasantly sandy track that goes through the trees; do not opt for the track a short way up the hillside which is for racehorses! The bridleway drops down to a small, isolated house at Nohome; here you follow the bridleway, turning uphill to the right on a narrow track which can be horribly muddy.

6. Follow this track to the road on the outskirts of Tadworth, taking a right and a left to go offroad once again. A sign for the Surrey Pony Club guarantees that this track is well used by horses, but conditions improve as you cross under the M25, riding through pretty woodland to emerge on the road at Headley.

7. Headley boasts village shops and an attractive pub. From here, turn north-west along the road, taking the first left turn on a narrow lane downhill, and then bearing off to the right on a clearly signposted bridleway. This leads past Nower Wood to the B2033; turn right here, then left by a car park onto the next bridleway, taking the left-hand fork to White Hill.

8. This is another fine track which speeds you to the top of White Hill in memorable surroundings. If you've had enough, the bridleway goes straight on to rejoin the outward route at the top of Mickleham Downs; however, if you're an adventurous rider, the best of the route is still to come, with an unsignposted left turn (bridleway) taking you downhill – it gets steep and then very steep, until it's a matter of technique to be able to stay in the saddle.

9. At the bottom there is another small car park, with the bridleway continuing up the opposite hillside by the side of a small house.

This is a fairly steep climb up to High Ashurst Youth Centre, where there is a choice of tarmac lane or offroad track heading south along the top towards Box Hill. The track is more fun; in fact this area is so good that when you reach the outskirts of Box Hill (where the houses begin) it's worth diverting onto the bridleway that turns eastwards. This gives a fine up-and-down ride on the south side of Headley Heath; then you turn south onto a track that leads to the road close to Maybury Farm.

10. Turn right along the road, following it past Box Hill and onto the next small settlement, where a bridleway turns right into the woods by the side of a caravan park. This is another excellent, well-signposted track which follows Lodge Hill, breaking out of the woods for a wonderful downhill through a steep gulley, then reaching the road a short distance east of Juniper Hall.

From here, turn left and left again, following the road down towards Burford Bridge. On the way down you may wish to investigate the bridleway which leads to the top of Box Hill Country Park; if you do so, show consideration to walkers who throng the hillside.

Keep off the 'gallops', which are all around the Epsom race course.

Places To Visit:
Box Hill Country Park
(tel: 01306 885502);
Denbies Vineyard
(tel: 01306 876616);
Epsom Racecourse.

Top Pubs:
The Cock at Headley.

Cycling Books from the Crowood Press

Great Cycle Routes – Cumbria and North Yorkshire   Jeremy Evans

Great Cycle Routes – Dartmoor and Exmoor   Jeremy Evans

Great Cycle Routes – Dorset and the New Forest   Jeremy Evans

Great Cycle Routes – Wales and the Borders   Jeremy Evans

50 Mountain Bike Rides   Jeremy Evans

Adventure Mountain Biking   Carlton Reid

Cycle Sport   Peter Konopka

Offroad Adventure Cycling   Jeremy Evans

Touring Bikes   Tony Oliver

Mountain Biking – The Skills of the Game   Paul Skilbeck